PIANO • VOCAL • CHORDS

WORLD'S GREATEST
CHRISTMAS MUSIC

55 of the Most Popular Holiday Songs and Solos

T0055433

Celebrate the season with dozens of beloved Christmas songs from throughout the ages! Packed with traditional carols, festive standards, and holiday hits, this sheet music anthology promises a lifetime of music-making fun for all occasions, from family sing-alongs to Christmas concerts.

ISBN-13: 978-0-7390-6284-5

EXCLUSIVELY DISTRIBUTED BY

HAL•LEONARD®

CONTENTS

Title	Page
All I Want for Christmas Is You	10
Angels We Have Heard on High	4
Believe	6
Celebrate Me Home	13
The Christmas Blues	18
Christmas Canon	24
Christmas Eve / Sarajevo 12/24	29
The Christmas Shoes	36
The Christmas Waltz	50
Coming Home for Christmas	44
Deck the Hall	60
Ding Dong Merrily on High	53
Do They Know It's Christmas?	62
Felíz Navidad	70
The First Noel	67
Frosty the Snowman	74
The Gift	77
Go Tell It on the Mountain	82
God Is With Us	84
Grown-Up Christmas List	91
Hallelujah! Chorus	96
Hark! The Herald Angels Sing	104
Have Yourself a Merry Little Christmas	108
Here We Come a-Caroling	106
(There's No Place Like) Home for the Holidays	111
I Want an Old-Fashioned Christmas	114
I'll Be Home for Christmas	118

It's the Most Wonderful Time of the Year 121
Jingle Bell Rock 124
Jingle Bells 127
Joy to the World 130
Last Christmas 132
Let It Snow! Let It Snow! Let It Snow! 138
Let There Be Peace on Earth 141
The Little Drummer Boy 144
The Little Drummer Boy / Peace on Earth 148
The Marvelous Toy 158
Mary, Did You Know? 160
Nativity Carol 164
O Christmas Tree (O Tannenbaum) 166
O Holy Night (Cantique de Noël) 168
O Little Town of Bethlehem 172
The Prayer 174
Santa Baby 182
Santa Claus Is Comin' to Town 186
Silent Night 191
Sleigh Ride 192
These Are the Special Times 153
The Twelve Days of Christmas 198
We Wish You a Merry Christmas 206
Wexford Carol 214
When Christmas Comes to Town 208
Winter Wonderland 219
Wizards in Winter 226
You're a Mean One, Mr. Grinch 224

ANGELS WE HAVE HEARD ON HIGH

TRADITIONAL

© 2009 ALFRED MUSIC PUBLISHING CO., INC.
All Rights Reserved

Chorus:
G E Am D/F♯ Em C
Glo -
Dsus D G D G Am/C G/D D G E
ri - a in ex - cel - sis De - o. Glo -
Am D Em C A7/C♯ Dsus D
ri - a
1.2.3. 4.
G D G Am/C G/D D G G
in ex - cel - sis De - o. o.

From THE POLAR EXPRESS

BELIEVE

Words and Music by
ALAN SILVESTRI and GLEN BALLARD

© 2004 HAZEN MUSIC, JOBANALA MUSIC and AEROSTATION CORPORATION
All Rights for HAZEN MUSIC Administered by WB MUSIC CORP.
All Rights Reserved

E
G♯m/D♯
E
G♯m/D♯
We were dream - ers, not so long a - go,
Ships go sail - ing far a - cross the sea,
F♯m
E♭
F♯m
A
B
but one by one, we all had to grow up.
trust - ing star - light to get where they need to be.
G♯m
A
D/F♯
When it seems the mag - ic slipped a - way, we find it all a - gain on Christ-mas
When it seems that we have lost our way, we find our-selves a - gain on Christ-mas
mf
1. To Next Strain
2.
Chorus:
Bsus
B
Bsus
B
E
F♯m11
Day. Be - Day. Be - lieve in what your heart is say-ing,
cresc.

E(9)/G♯
A
E
B(4)/D♯
hear the mel - o - dy that's play-ing. There's no time to waste, there's so
F♯m7
E/B
Bsus
E
F♯m11
much to cel - e - brate. Be - lieve in what you feel in - side and
E(9)/G♯
G♯7(♯5)
C♯m
give your dreams the wings to fly.
F♯m7
B7sus
1.
E
G♯m/D♯
You have ev - 'ry - thing you need if you just be - lieve.
8va

2.
E F♯m11 E(9)/G♯ A E B(4)/D♯ F♯m7 E/B Bsus
be-lieve. If you just be-lieve, if you just
be-lieve, if you just be-lieve. Just be-
lieve, just be-lieve.
Repeat ad lib. and fade

ALL I WANT FOR CHRISTMAS IS YOU

(A Christmas Love Song)

Lyrics by
ALAN and MARILYN BERGMAN

Music by
JOHNNY MANDEL

© 1988, 1991 THREESOME MUSIC CO. and MARISSA MUSIC
All Rights Reserved

B
E♭6/9
A♭Ma9
GMa7
Em7
All I need for Christ - mas is here. Find - ing
Ped.
sim.
Am7
A♭+/A
C/D
D13 D9(+5)
G6/D
Em7
ev - 'ry sweet sur - prise wrapped up in your eyes, wait - ing there for me
Fm7
B♭13
B♭7+(♯9/♭9)
C
B♭m9
E♭9
B♭m7
E♭13(♭9)
un - der - neath the tree. We'll spend the day ex - chang - ing
A♭Ma7
A♭6
A♭Ma7
Fm7
D♭13
B♭/C
C7(♭9/+5) C7(♭9)
kiss - es. Smile and say "What a
8va

E♭/F F13 C♭7 A♭/B♭ F♭7/B♭ D E♭6/9 A♭Maj9
Christ - mas this is!" Long be - fore the snow - flakes ap -
Gm7 Cm7 Fm7 C+/F A♭/B♭ B♭13
pear, with - out bells or mis - tle - toe or the
Gm7 C13 Gm7 C9 E♭/F F9 A♭/B♭ B♭13 B♭7(♭9/+5)
tin - sel's sil - ver glow, you just look at me and oh, Christ - mas is
poco rall.
last x rall.
1. E♭6/9 Fm7 A♭/B♭ A♭o/B♭
here!
2. E♭6/9
here!
8va
rall.
Ped.
Ped.

CELEBRATE ME HOME

Lyrics by
KENNY LOGGINS

Music by
KENNY LOGGINS and BOB JAMES

© 1977 (Renewed) MILK MONEY MUSIC
All Rights Reserved

G7sus4
G7
B♭/C
F
Am7
Dm7
Gm7
3fr.
Oh, my friends.
Please cel-e-brate me home.
C
C♯o7
3fr.
Dm
Am
Gm
3 fr.
C
B♭maj7
Gim-me a num-ber. Please cel-e-brate me home. Play me one more song that I'll
Am7
Dm
Dm(maj7)
F/G
G9
B♭/C
al-ways re-mem-ber; that I can re-call when-ev-er I find my-self too all a-
C
Em7-5
F
E♭6/9/F
B♭6/9/F
E♭7
4 fr.
lone. I can sing me home.

F
Bb/F
C/E
F
Bb/F
C/E
Un-eas-y high-way, trav-'lin' where the west-er-ly winds can fly.
Dm
G7sus4
G7
Gm7/C
Bb/C
Am7/C
Bb/C
Some-bod-y tried to tell me. But the man for-got to tell me why.
F
Bb/F
C/E
F
Cm/Eb
I got to count on be-ing gone. Come on, Ma-ma. Come on, Dad-dy. And
cresc.
mf
Dm9
Bm7-5
E7
Am
Cm7
F7-9
Bbm9
please, what do you want from me? I'll be strong.

F♭maj7
A♭m7/D♭
B♭/C
I'll be weak. I'll be weak.
cresc.
F
Am7
Dm7
Gm7
3 fr.
C
C♯o7
3fr.
Dm
Am
Please cel-e-brate me home. Gim-me a num-ber. Please cel-e-brate me
f
Gm
3fr.
C
B♭maj7
Am7
home. Play me one more song that I'll al-ways re-mem-ber;
Dm
Dm(maj7)
F/G
G9
B♭/C
that I can re-call when-ev-er I find my-self too all a-lone.

Cm7
3fr.
C/E
I can make be-lieve I've nev-er gone. Lem-me, lem-me know where I be-long. Sing me
F
Am7
Dm7
Gm7
3fr.
C
C♯o7
3fr.
Dm
Am
Please
home. cel-e-brate me home. Gim-me a num-ber. Please cel-e-brate me
Gm
3fr.
C
B♭maj7
Am7
Gm7
3fr
B♭/C
F
Gm7
F/A
home. Play me one more song, y'all. Well, I'm
15ma
loco
sub. pp
mp
Repeat and fade
B♭maj7
Am7
Gm7
3fr.
B♭/C
F
Gm7
F/A
fi-n'lly here. But I'm bound to roam. Come on, cel-e-brate me home. Well, I'm

THE CHRISTMAS BLUES

Words by
SAMMY CAHN

Music by
DAVID HOLT

© 1953 (Renewed) CAHN MUSIC CO. and TEN/FOUR MUSIC COMPANY
All Rights Administered by WB MUSIC CORP.
All Rights Reserved

G7
D
C7
B7
sure that you'll for - give me if I don't en - thuse. I
E7
G/A
A7
F♯7
B7
E7
A7
guess I've got the Christ - mas blues. 2. I've
Verse 2:
Dmaj7
Em7
Dmaj7
Em7
done my win - dow shop - ping, there's not a store I've missed. But
Dm7
Em7
F♯m7
Gmaj7
C/D
D7
what's the use of stop - ping when there's no one on your list? You'll

G7
D
C7
B7
know the way I'm feel - ing when you love and you lose. I
E7
G/A
A7
D6
A11
D6
guess I've got the Christ - mas blues. When
Bridge:
F♯m7
B7
F♯m7
B7
Em
C/E
some - bod - y wants you, some-bod - y needs you, Christ-mas is a joy of
Em7
G♯m7
C♯7
joy. But, friends, when you're lone - ly,

G♯m7
C♯7
F♯m7(♭5)
B7
Em7
A9
you'll find that it's on - ly a thing for lit - tle girls and lit - tle boys.
3. May
Verse 3:
Dmaj7
Em7
Dmaj7
Gmaj7/A
all your days be mer - ry, your sea - sons full of cheer. But
Dmaj7
Em7
F♯m7
Gmaj7
C/D
D7
'til it's Jan - u - ar - y I'll just go and dis - ap - pear. Oh,
G7
D
C7
B7
San - ta may have brought you some stars for your shoes, but

E7sus E7 A7sus A7 F♯m7(♭5) B9 E7(♭5) E7 E7(♭5) E7
San - ta on - ly brought me the blues, those bright - ly pack-aged, tin - sel cov - ered
Gmaj7/A D6 G7 F♯7 B7 E7 A7
Christ - mas blues.
Dmaj7 Em7 Dmaj7 Gmaj7/A
Dmaj7 Em7 F♯m7 Gmaj7 F♯m7 Em7 C/D D7
Oh,

G7
D
C7
B7
San - ta may have brought you some stars for your shoes, but
E7sus
E7
A7sus
A7
F♯m7(♭5)
B9
San - ta on - ly brought me the blues, those
E7(♭5)
E7
E7(♭5)
E7
Gmaj7/A
bright - ly pack - aged, tin - sel cov - ered Christ - mas
D6
G7
F♯7
B13(♯11)
E7(♯9)
A7(♯9)
E♭9(♯11)
D6/9
blues.
(straight 8ths)
rall.

CHRISTMAS CANON

Words and Music by
PAUL O'NEILL

© 1998 WARNER-TAMERLANE PUBLISHING CORP. and PAUL O'NEILL PUBLISHING
All Rights Administered by WARNER-TAMERLANE PUBLISHING CORP.
All Rights Reserved

D A Bm F♯m G D G A
mp
D A Bm F♯m G D G A
D A Bm F♯m G D G A
Smoothly ♩ = 66
D A Bm F♯m
mf
G D G A

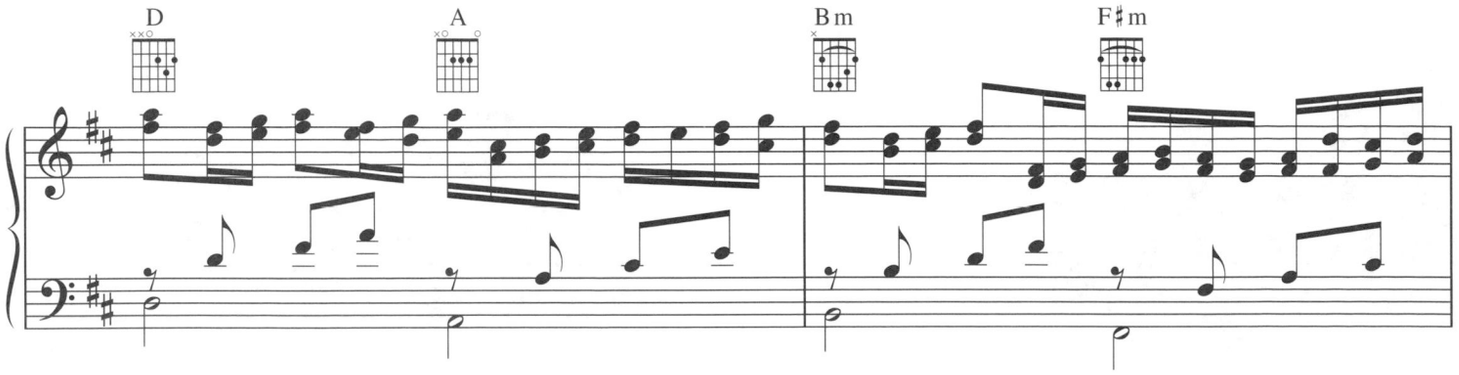
D
A
Bm
F♯m

To Coda 𝄌

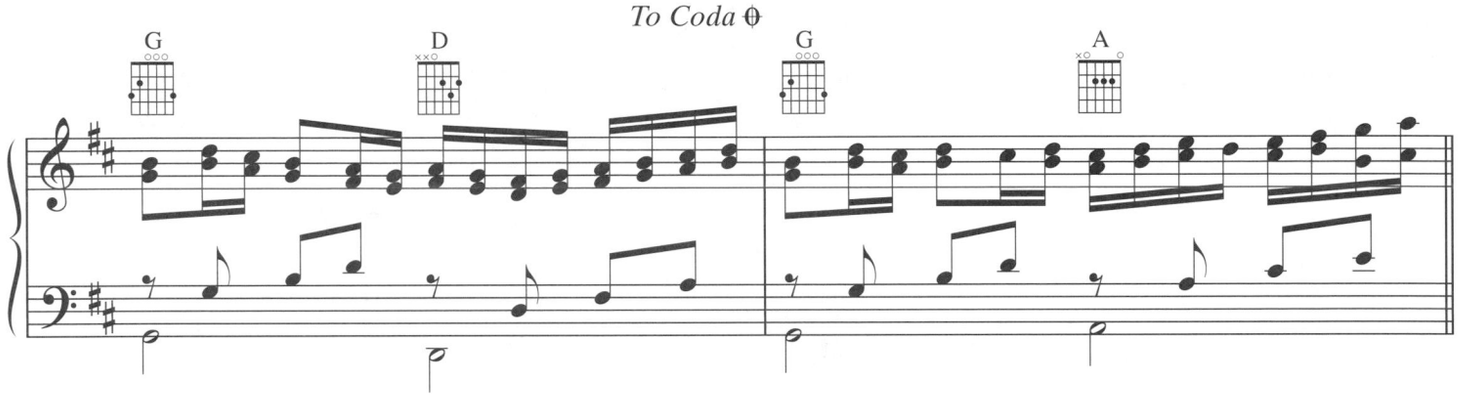
G
D
G
A

D
A
Bm
F♯m
G
D
G
A
This night we pray our lives will show this dream He had each child still knows.

D
A
Bm
F♯m
G
D
G
A
This night we pray our lives will show this dream He had each child still knows.

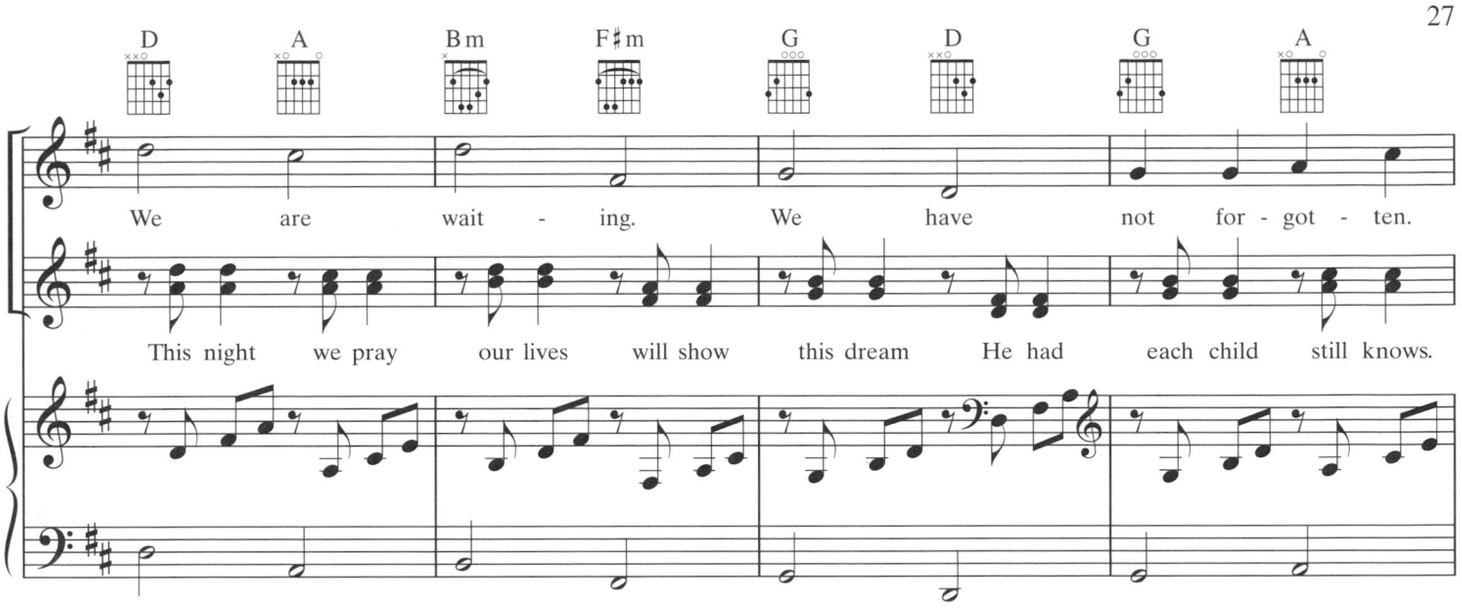
D A Bm F♯m G D G A
We are wait - ing. We have not for - got - ten.
This night we pray our lives will show this dream He had each child still knows.

D A Bm F♯m G D G A
We are wait - ing. We have not for - got - ten.
This night we pray our lives will show this dream He had each child still knows.

D A Bm F♯m
On this night, on this night, on this ver - y Christ - mas night. On this night, on this night, on this ver - y Christ - mas
We are wait - ing.
This night we pray our lives will show

G D G A
night. On this night, on this night, on this ver - y Christ - mas night. On this night, on this night, on this ver - y Christ-mas
We have not for - got - ten.
this dream He had each child still knows.
D A Bm F♯m G D G Asus A
night.
D.S.𝄋 al Coda
D A Bm F♯m G D G A
𝄌 Coda
G A D
molto rit.

CHRISTMAS EVE/SARAJEVO 12/24

Music by
PAUL O'NEILL and ROBERT KINKEL

© 1997 WARNER-TAMERLANE PUBLISHING CORP., PAUL O'NEILL PUBLISHING and ROBERT STELLER PUBLISHING
All Rights Administered by WARNER-TAMERLANE PUBLISHING CORP.
All Rights Reserved

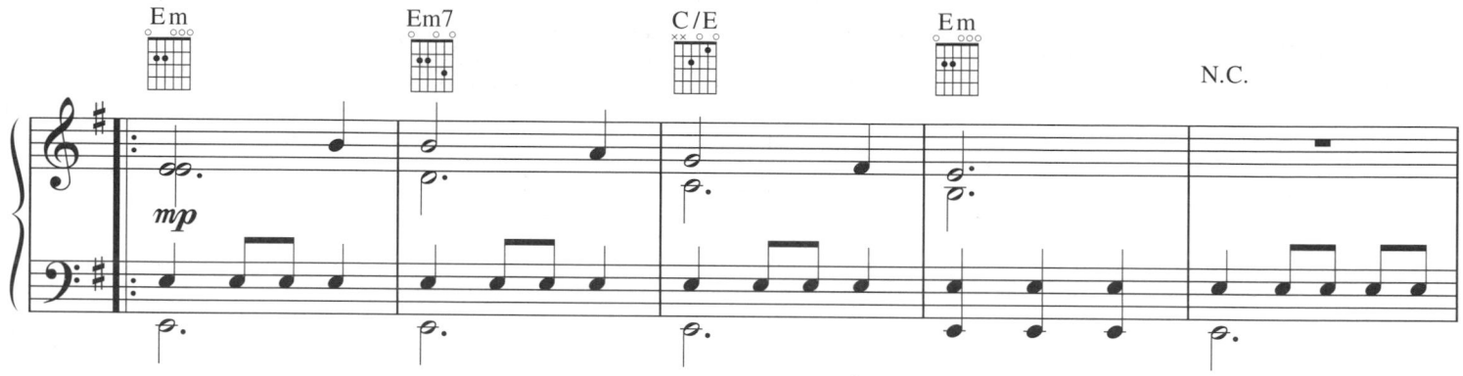
Em
Em7
C/E
Em
N.C.
mp

1.
2.

Em
mf

cresc.

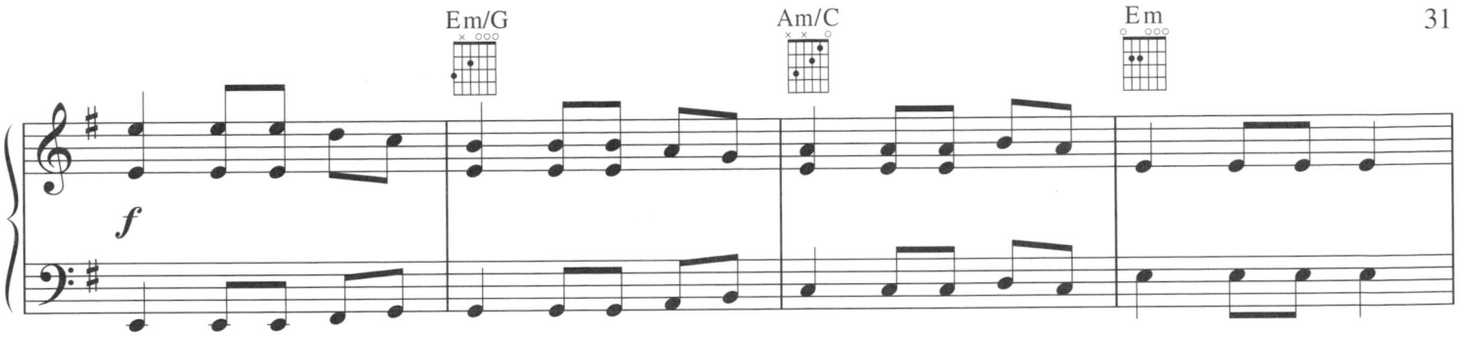
Em/G
Am/C
Em
f

B 5
f

N.C.
ff

N.C.
dim.
p
Em
Em7
C/E
Em
C/E
Em7
Am7
cresc. poco a poco
Em
Am7
Em
Am7
Em
Am7
Em
mf
sempre cresc.

Am7
Em
N.C.
f
sub. mp
Em
Em7
C/E
Em
mf
C/E
Em7
Am7/E
E5
Am7/E
Em
Am7/E
cresc. poco a poco
Em
C/E
Em7
Am7/E
Em
Em
Em/G
ff
Am/C
Em
B5

Am7/E
N.C.
Am7/E
N.C.
pp
ff
pp
ff
Em
Em/G
Am/C
Em
B5
ff
cresc.
Em
Em/D
C
Em/B
fff
Em
Em/D
C
Em/B

Em
N.C.
ffff
E5
Em

THE CHRISTMAS SHOES

Words and Music by
LEONARD AHLSTROM and
EDDIE CARSWELL

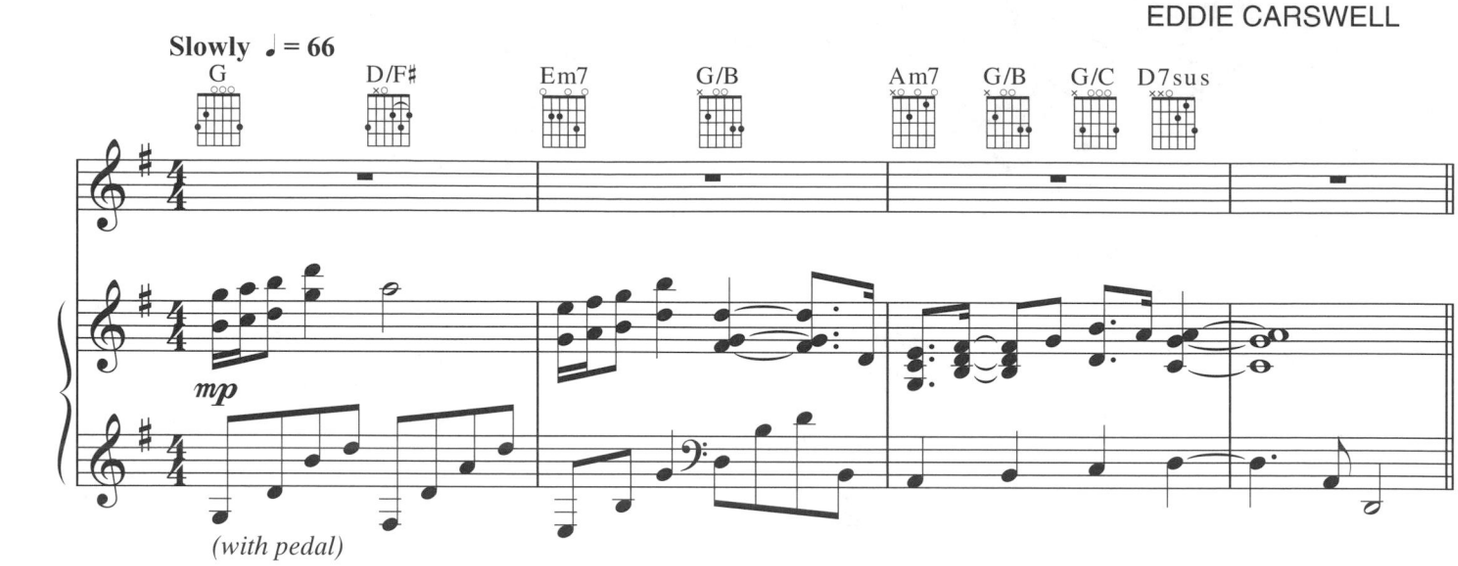

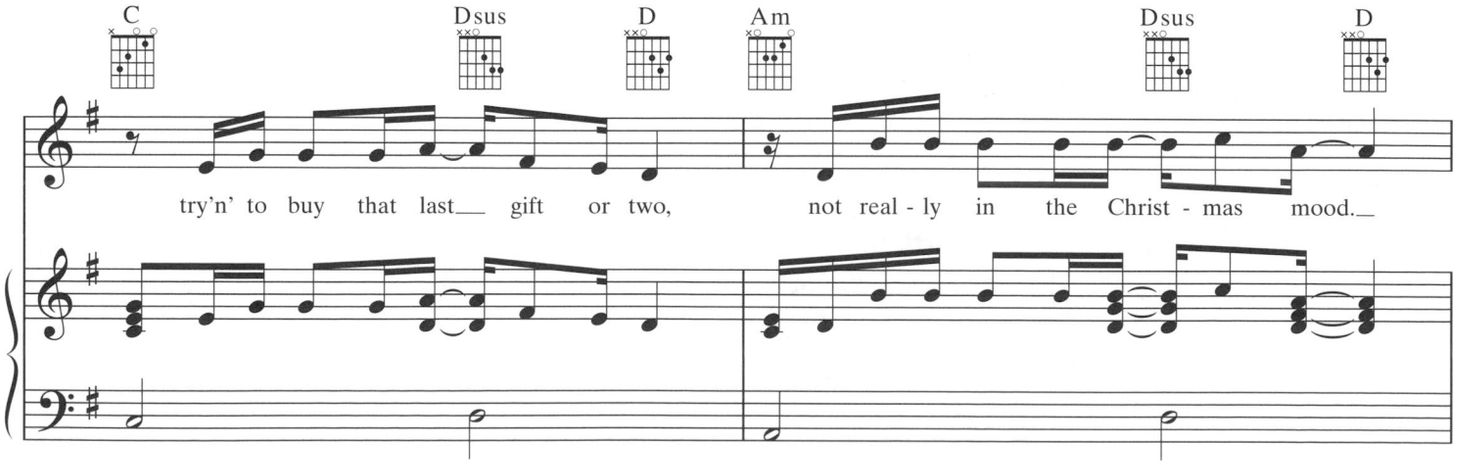

© 2000 WB MUSIC CORP., JERRY HAVEN MUSIC and SONY ATV SONGS LLC, d/b/a TREE PUBLISHING CO.
All Rights on behalf of itself and JERRY HAVEN MUSIC Administered by WB MUSIC CORP.
All Rights Reserved

G
G/F♯
Em7
G/D
Stand-ing right in front of me was a lit-tle boy wait-ing anx-ious-ly,
C
D7sus
D7
Am7
D7sus
D7
pac-ing 'round like lit-tle boys do and in his hands he held a pair of shoes.
G5
D/F♯
Em
G/D
And his clothes were worn and old. He was
Em
G/D
C
G/B
dirt-y from head to toe. And when it came his time to pay, I

G/C
D7sus
D7
could - n't be - lieve what I heard him say. Sir, I wan - na
Chorus:
A
E
F♯m7
E
buy these shoes for my Ma - ma, please. It's
mf
D
E7sus
E7
A
F♯m
E
Christ-mas Eve and these shoes are just her size. Could you
A
E
F♯m7
E
hur - ry, Sir, Dad - dy says there's not much time. You see,

D
E7sus
E7
D
E7sus
E7
Mom's been sick for quite a while. And I know these shoes would make her smile. And I
D
E7sus
E7
Bm7
C♯m7
D2
E7sus
want her to look beau - ti - ful if Ma - ma meets Je - sus to -
A
E/G♯
F♯m7
D
E7sus
night.
2. He count - ed
Verse 2:
A
A/G♯
F♯m7
A/E
pen - nies for what seemed like years. Then the cash - ier said, "Son, there's not e - nough here."

D
Esus
E
Bm7
Esus
E
He searched his pock - ets fran - ti - c'lly, then he turned and he looked at me. He said,
A
A/G♯
F♯m7
A/E
"Ma-ma made Christ-mas good at our house, though most years she just did with-out. Tell me,
D
E7sus
E7
Bm7
E7sus
E7
sir, what am I gon - na do? Some - how I've got to buy her these Christ-mas
A
F♯m7
A/E
shoes." So I laid the mon - ey down. I just

F♯m7
A/E
D
A/C♯
had to help him out. And I'll nev-er for-get the look on his face when he said,
A/D
E7sus
E7
"Ma-ma's gon-na look so great." Sir, I wan-na
Chorus:
B
F♯
G♯m7
F♯
buy these shoes for my Ma-ma, please. It's
a tempo
E
F♯7sus
F♯7
B
G♯m
F♯
Christ-mas Eve and these shoes are just her size. Could you

B
F♯
G♯m7
F♯
hur - ry, Sir, Dad - dy says there's not much time. You see,
E
F♯
E
F♯
Mom's been sick for quite a while. And I know these shoes would make her smile. And I
To Coda
E
F♯
C♯m7
D♯m7
E2
F♯7sus
want her to look beau - ti - ful if Ma - ma meets Je - sus to -
Bridge:
B
F♯/B
B
C♯m7
B/D♯
night. I knew I caught a glimpse of heav - en's love as he

F♯
G♯m7
A
E/G♯
thanked me and ran out. I knew that God had sent that lit - tle boy to re -
F♯sus
F♯
freely
C♯m9
F♯sus
D.S. 𝄋 al Coda
mind me what Christ-mas is all a - bout. Sir, I want to
rit.
Coda
B2
E
F♯sus
F♯
C♯m7
D♯m7
B/E
F♯sus
night. I want her to look beau - ti - ful if Ma - ma meets Je - sus to -
B
F♯/A♯
G♯m7
E2
B(9)
night.
a tempo
rit.

COMING HOME FOR CHRISTMAS

Words and Music by
JIM BRICKMAN, VICTORIA SHAW
and RICHIE McDONALD

© 2007 UNIVERSAL TUNES, a division of UNIVERSAL INC. / BRICKMAN SONGS (SESAC),
AVARU MUSIC, INC. / MULTISONGS, a division of BMG (SESAC) and LOREMOMA MUSIC (BMI)
Worldwide Print Rights for BRICKMAN SONGS Administered by ALFRED MUSIC PUBLISHING CO., INC.
All Rights Reserved

Verses 2 & 3:
C
F(9)
Csus
C
F(9)
2. If I could make this plane go an - y fast - er,
3. Ev - 'ry - where I go, it makes me miss you,
Am7
F(9)
Gsus
G
I'd be stand - ing right out - side your door.
'cause ev - 'ry-where I look, it's red and green.
Ev - 'ry -
Am
F(9)
C
G/B
Am7
C/G
I can close my eyes and see that sweet look of sur - prise there on
bod - y cel - e - brat - ing on - ly makes the wait - ing slow
Dm7
F(9)
your face. It's worth the wait.
down the day. I'm on my way.
Hang the

Chorus:
G
Am7
G/B
C(9)
mis - tle - toe by the fire's glow, put the an - gel on the tree. Light a
Am7
G/B
Dsus
D
can - dle in the win - dow, just for me. I'll
G
Am7
G/B
bring you all my heart and soul, my love, my hugs and
C
Cm/E♭
G(9)/B
Em7
kiss - es. I'm com - ing home, I'm com - ing

Am7
D7sus
1.
Gsus2 sus4
G
home for Christ - mas.
C
F(9)
2.
Gsus2 sus4
G(9)
Christ - mas.
Bridge:
C2
G/B
Wan - na hear all a - bout all the things you're do - ing and
Am7
Em7
G
C2
G/B
make up for lost time.
Tell you what I've been through, laugh like we al - ways do.

Am7
Dsus
D
God, I've been miss - ing you. Hang the
Chorus:
G
Am7
G/B
C(9)
mis - tle - toe by the fire's glow, put the an - gel on the tree. Light a
mp
Am7
G/B
Dsus
D7
can - dle in the win - dow, just for me. I'll
G
Am7
G/B
bring you all my heart and soul, my love, my hugs and
mf

C
Cm/E♭
G/B
Em7
kiss - es.
I'm com - ing home.
You won't be a - lone.
Am7
G/B
Dsus
I'm com - ing home for
8va
decresc.
G sus2 sus4
G
C(9)
F(9)
Christ - mas.
poco rit.
a tempo
Am
F(9)
C/G
G7sus
C(9)
rit.

THE CHRISTMAS WALTZ

Words by
SAMMY CAHN

Music by
JULE STYNE

© 1954 SANDS MUSIC CORP.
Copyright Renewed and Assigned to CAHN MUSIC COMPANY and JULE STYNE
JULE STYNE'S interest Controlled by PRODUCERS MUSIC PUBL. CO., INC. and Administered by CHAPPELL & CO., INC.
All Rights Reserved

Gm7
C7-9
Fmaj7
Dm7
G9
G7-5
filled his sleigh with things, Things for you and for
C7
C7+5
F
D7sus4
D7
Gm7
me. It's that time of year, When the world falls in
C7
F
D7-9
love, Ev - 'ry song you hear seems to
Gm
C7-9
F
say: "Mer - ry Christ - mas, May your

Gm7
C7
Am7-5
D7
D+
D7
New Year dreams come true. "
And this
G9
C9
C7
F
song of mine,
in three - quar - ter time,
D7
G7
Cm7
C7
Wish - es you and yours
the same thing
F
Dm
Gm7
C9
F
too.
poco rall.

DING DONG MERRILY ON HIGH

Traditional,
Arranged by DAVID DOWNES

© 2006 LIFFEY PUBLISHING LTD, Dublin 2, Ireland
All Rights Reserved Used by Permission

D2/A
Amaj7/E
E7/D
A
D/A
Glo
-
Ding, dong, dong. Ding, dong, dong,
cresc.
mf
A
D/A
E7/A
A
Bm/A
E/A
D
E7
A5
ri - a, Ho - san - na in ex - cel - sis.
ding, dong, dong, ding, dong, dong. Ho - san - na in ex - cel - sis.
A
D/A
A
Bm/A
E/A
Glo
-
Ding, dong, dong, ding, dong, dong,

A
Bm/A
E/A
D
E7
A
ri - a, Ho - san - na in ex - cel - sis.
Violin
ding, dong, dong. Ho - san - na in ex - cel - sis.
A5
D2
A
Bm7(4)
Esus
A
D
E/B
A
1. E'en so here be - low, be - low, let stee - ple bells be swung - en.
2. Pray you, du - ti - ful - ly prime, your mat - in chime, ye ring - ers.
D
E/B
A
And i - o, i - o, i - o, by priest and peo - ple sung - en.
May you beau - ti - ful - ly rhyme your eve - time song, ye sing - ers.

A/E D/E A/E D/E E A/E Bm/E E
Glo - ri - a, Ho -
D A/E F♯m7 E/G♯ A D/A A D/A E/A
san - na in ex - cel - sis. Glo -
Ding, dong, dong, ding, dong, dong,
A D E
1.
D E A
ri - a, Ho - san - na in ex - cel - sis.
ding, dong, dong. Ho - san - na in ex - cel - sis.

2.
D
E7
F♯m7
E/G♯
A5
Asus
san-na in ex-cel - sis.
san-na in ex-cel - sis.
A
Asus
E5
E7sus
A/E
E7sus
Bm7
C♯m
D

58
N.C.
Glo - ri - a, ri - a,
Glo - ri - a, ri - a,
Glo - ri - a, glo - ri -
p
D E/D A/D D E/D A/D D E/D
a.
Ding, dong, dong, ding, dong, dong, ding, dong, dong,
cresc.
mf
A/E E D/E E7 F♯m7 A/G♯ A D/A
Ho - san - na in ex - cel - sis. Glo -
ding, dong, dong. Ho - san - na in ex - cel - sis. Ding, dong, dong,

A D/A E/A A Bm/D E D E7 F♯m7 A/G♯
ri - a, Ho - san - na in ex - cel - sis.
ding, dong, dong, ding, dong, dong. Ho - san - na in ex - cel - sis.
A D/A A D/A E/A
Glo -
Ding, dong, dong, ding, dong, dong,
A/C♯ Bm/D E D E7 A
ri - a, Ho - san - na in ex - cel - sis.
ding, dong, dong. Ho - san - na in ex - cel - sis.
molto rit.

DECK THE HALL

TRADITIONAL

© 2009 ALFRED MUSIC PUBLISHING CO., INC.
All Rights Reserved

C7 F C F C7 F C7
Fa la la la la la la la la.
Don we now our
Fol - low me in
Sing we joy - ous
F C Dm7 G7 C G7 C7
gay ap - par - el.
mer - ry mea - sure,
all to - geth - er,
Fa la la la la la la la la.
F C7 F C7 Dm C7 F B♭ F Gm7
Troll the an - cient Yule - tide car - ol.
while I tell of Yule - tide trea - sure.
heed - less of the wind and weath - er.
Fa la la la la la
1.2.
F C7 F
la la la.
3.
F C7 F
la la la.
rit.

DO THEY KNOW IT'S CHRISTMAS?

(Feed the World)

Medium Rock

Words and Music by
BOB GELDOF and MIDGE URE

© 1985 CHAPPELL MUSIC, LTD.
All Rights in the U.S. Administered by WB MUSIC CORP.
All Rights Reserved

F
Dm
G6
C
Throw your arms a - round the world at Christ - mas - time.
F
G
C
But say a prayer, to pray for the oth - er ones
F
G
C
at Christ - mas - time. It's hard, but when you're hav - ing fun
F
G
C
there's a world out - side your win - dow, and it's a world of dread and fear

F Dm7 G C
where the on - ly wa - ter flow - ing is the bit - ter sting of
F Dm7 G C
tears. And the Christ - mas bells that ring there are the clang - ing chimes of doom.
F Dm7 G C
Well, to - night thank God it's them in - stead of you.
Csus C F G C
And there won't be snow in Af - ri - ca this Christ - mas - time,

F G C
the great-est gift they'll get this year is life. Oh.
Dm/C C F G C
Where noth-ing ev-er grows, no rain or riv-ers flow,
F Dm7 F/G C
do they know it's Christ-mas-time at all?
F C Am G Am G
Here's to you, raise a glass for ev'-ry-one; here's to them un-der-neath that burn-ing sun.

F
F/G
C
F
C/E
F
C/E
Do they know it's Christ-mas-time at__ all?
Dm7
Dm7/G
C
F
C/E
F
C/E
Dm7
Dm7/G
Feed the world.____
C
F
C/E
F
Am/E
Dm7
Dm7/G
Feed the world,____ let them know it's Christ - mas - time a -
C
F
C/E
F
Am/E
Dm7
Dm7/G
Feed the world,____
Repeat and Fade
gain. let them know it's Christ - mas - time a -

THE FIRST NOEL

TRADITIONAL

© 2009 ALFRED MUSIC PUBLISHING CO., INC.
All Rights Reserved

D Bm A Em/G D/F♯ G
fields where they lay keep - ing their
to the earth, it gave great
seek for a King was their in -
there it did both stop and
of - fered there in His pres -
hath made heav'n and earth of

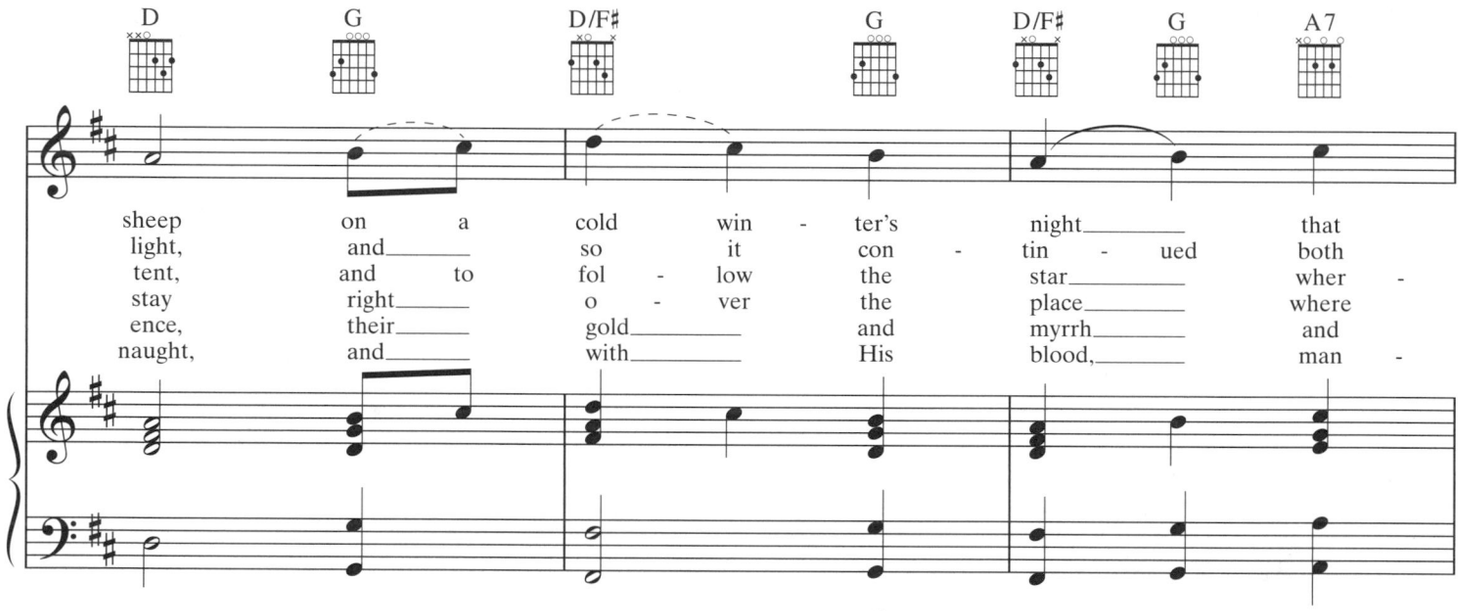
D G D/F♯ G D/F♯ G A7
sheep on a cold win - ter's night that
light, and so it con - tin - ued both
tent, and to fol - low the star wher -
stay right o - ver the place where
ence, their gold and myrrh and
naught, and with His blood, man -

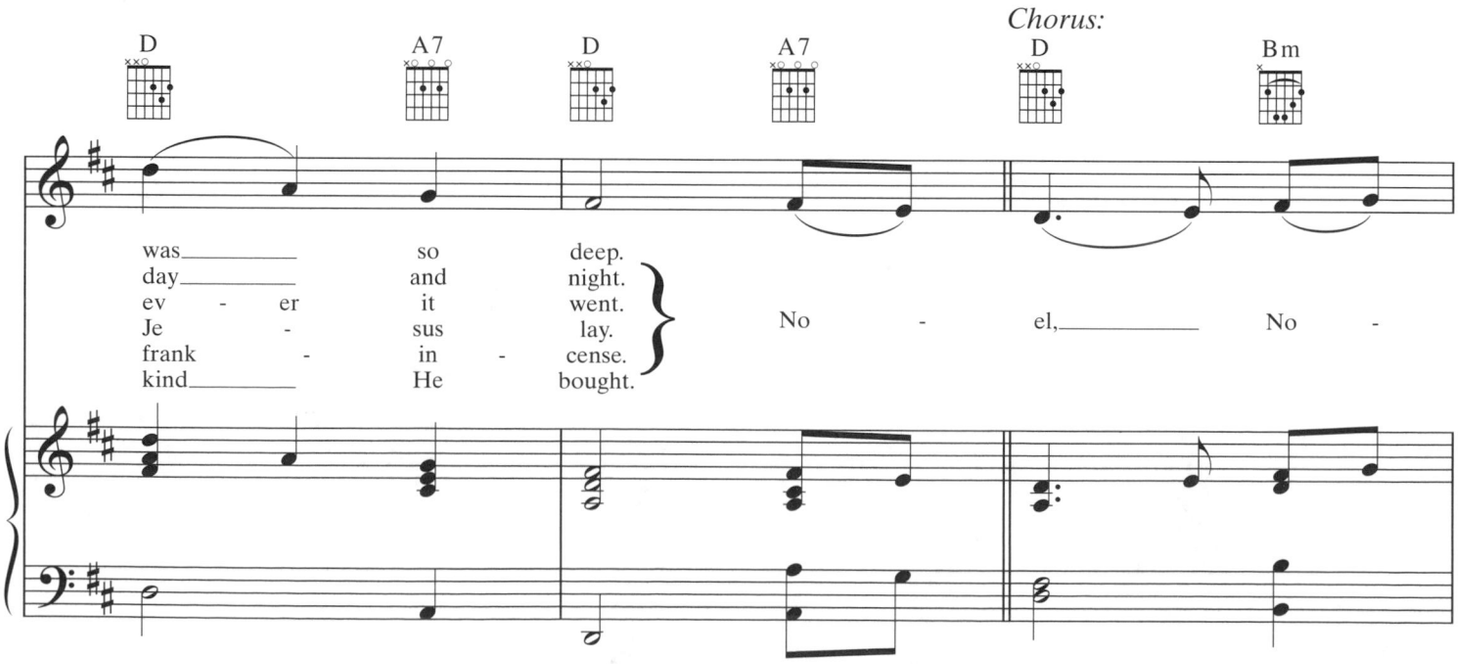
Chorus:
D A7 D A7 D Bm
was so deep.
day and night.
ev - er it went.
Je - sus lay.
frank - in - cense.
kind He bought.
No - el, No -

F♯m
D/F♯
G
D
A/C♯
el, No - el, No - el,
B m
F♯m/A
G
D
A7
D/F♯
A7
born is the King of Is - ra -
1.–5.
6.
D
D
el.
2. They
3. And
4. This
5. Then
6. Then
el.

FELIZ NAVIDAD

Words and Music by
JOSÉ FELICIANO

© 1970 (Renewed) J & H PUBLISHING COMPANY
All Rights Reserved Used by Permission

A7
D
N.C.
- ño y fe - li - ci - dad.
Fe - liz Na - vi -
G
A7
D
dad.
Fe - liz Na - vi - dad.
G
A7
Fe - liz Na - vi - dad.
Pros - pe - ro a - ño y fe - li - ci - dad.
Chorus:
D
N.C.
G
I want to wish you a Mer - ry Christ - mas.
f

A7
D
Bm7
I want to wish you a Mer - ry Christ - mas. I want to wish you a
G
A7
D
Mer - ry Christ - mas from the bot - tom of my heart.
N.C.
G
A7
I want to wish you a Mer - ry Christ - mas. I want to wish you a
D
Bm7
G
Mer - ry Christ - mas. I want to wish you a Mer - ry Christ - mas from the

A7
D
1.2.
N.C.
bot - tom of my heart.
Fe - liz Na - vi -
mf
3.
N.C.
G
A7
Fe - liz Na - vi - dad.
Fe - liz Na - vi -
mf
D
G
dad.
Fe - liz Na - vi - dad.
Pros - pe - ro a -
A7
D
ño y fe - li - ci - dad.

FROSTY THE SNOWMAN

Words and Music by
STEVE NELSON and JACK ROLLINS

© 1950 HILL AND RANGE SONGS, INC.
Copyright Renewed and Assigned to CHAPPELL & CO., INC.
All Rights Reserved

C C7 F F♯dim C
FROS - TY THE SNOW MAN is a fair - y tale they say, He was
Down to the vil - lage with a broom-stick in his hand, Run-ning
mf
F F♯dim C Am A7 Dm7 G7 C C7
made of snow but the chil-dren know how he came to life one day. There
here and there all a - round the square, say-in' "catch me if you can." He
F F♯dim C Dm7 G7 C Caug
must have been some mag - ic in that old silk hat they found. For
led them down the streets of town right to the traf - fic cop. And he
mp
G Ddim Am D7 G Gaug
when they placed it on his head he be - gan to dance a - round. Oh,
on - ly paused a mo - ment when he heard him hol - ler "stop"! For
cresc.

C
C7
F
F♯dim
C
FROS - TY THE SNOW MAN was a - live as he could be And the
FROS - TY THE SNOW MAN had to hur - ry on his way But he
f
F
F♯dim
C
Am
A7
Dm7
G7
C
G7
chil - dren say he could laugh and play just the same as you and me.
waved good - bye say - in', "Don't you cry, I'll be back a - gain some day."
C
G7
Thump-et - y thump thump, thump-et - y thump thump Look at Fros - ty go.
mf (lightly)
C
Thump-et - y thump thump, thump-et - y thump thump O - ver the hills of snow.
f
sfz

THE GIFT

Words and Music by
JIM BRICKMAN and
TOM DOUGLAS

© 1997 BRICKMAN ARRANGEMENT/MULTISONGS INC. (A Division of Careers BMG Music Publishing) and SONY/ATV SONGS LLC d/b/a TREE PUBLISHING CO.
Print Rights for BRICKMAN ARRANGEMENT Administered Worldwide by ALFRED MUSIC PUBLISHING CO., INC.
All Rights Reserved

Gm7 B♭/F E♭(9) B♭/D Cm7
You're the an-swer when I prayed_ I would find some - one, and, ba-by, I___ found you._
Chorus:
F7sus F7 B♭/D E♭(9) F7sus F7
___ And all I want___ is to hold___ you for - ev-er.___ And all I need_
B♭/D E♭(9) F7sus F7 B♭/D D7
___ is you more_ ev-'ry day.___ You saved my heart_ from be-ing
Gm B♭/F Em7(♭5) Cm7 B♭/D F7sus
bro-ken a - part.__ You gave your love a-way, and I'm thank-ful ev-'ry day for the

B♭(9)
F/A
Gm7
B♭/F
E♭(9)
gift.

Verse 2:

F(9)
C/E
Dm7
F/C
B♭(9)
F/A
He:
2. Watch - ing as you soft - ly sleep. What I'd give if I could keep just this mo - ment. If

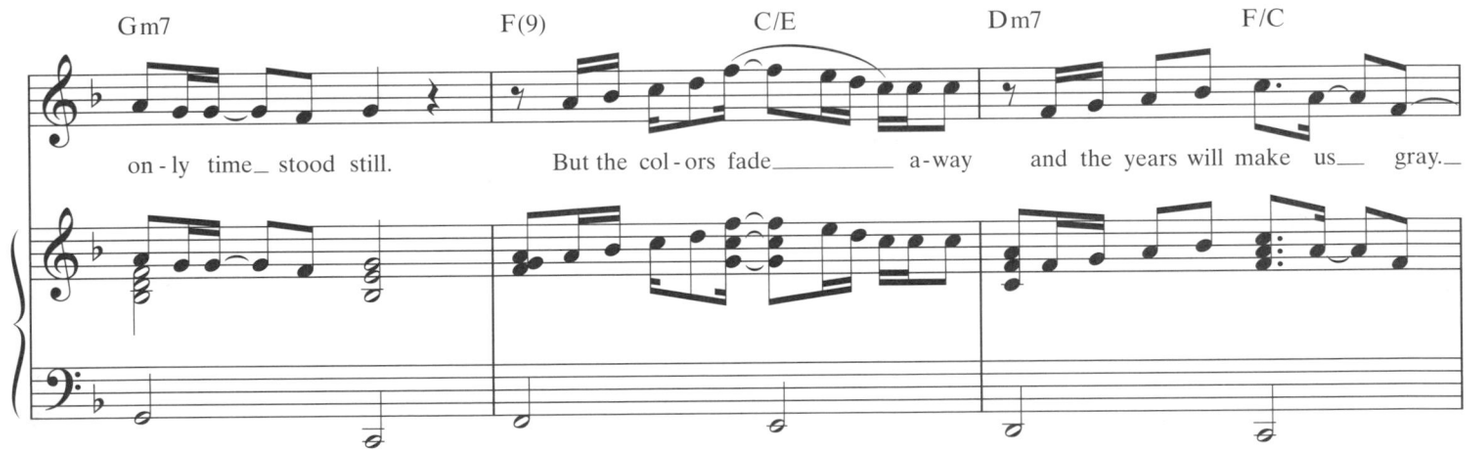
Gm7
F(9)
C/E
Dm7
F/C
on - ly time stood still. But the col - ors fade a - way and the years will make us gray.

B♭(9)
F/A
Gm7
C7sus
C7
Both:
But, ba - by, in my eyes, you'll still be beau - ti - ful. And all I want

Chorus:
F/A
B♭(9)
C7sus
C7
F/A
B♭(9)
is to hold you for - ev-er.
All I need is you more ev - 'ry
C7sus
C7
F/A
A7
To Coda
Dm
F/C
Bm7(♭5)
He:
She:
day.
You saved my heart from be-ing bro-ken a - part. You gave your
Gm7
F/A
C7sus
F
He:
Both:
love a - way,
and I'm thank - ful
ev-'ry day
for the
gift.
B♭(9)
C7sus
Dm7
F/A
B♭(9)
F/A
Gm7
C7sus
C7

D.S. 𝄋 al Coda
B♭(9)/D
C/E
F
B♭
Gm7
F/A
C7sus
C7
And all I want_
𝄌 Coda
Dm
F/C
Bm7(♭5)
Gm7
F/A
She:
He:
bro - ken a - part._____
You gave your love a - way.
I can't find the
B♭(9)
C/D
Dm7
Gm7
C7sus
F(9)
C/E
She:
Both:
words to say.
And I'm thank - ful ev - 'ry day_
for the gift.
rit.
a tempo
Dm7
F/C
B♭(9)
C7sus
F(9)
rit.

GO TELL IT ON THE MOUNTAIN

NEGRO SPIRITUAL

© 2009 ALFRED MUSIC PUBLISHING CO., INC.
All Rights Reserved

1.2.
C/G G Em A A7 A/C♯ D
hold, through - out the heav - ens there shone a ho - ly light.
out the an - gel cho - rus that hailed our Sav - ior's birth.
God sent us sal - va - tion that bless - ed Christ - mas
3.
D G Em D7 G/D G
morn. Go tell it on the moun - tain, o - ver the hills, and ev - 'ry - where.
mf
Em7 Am7 G/D D7 G
Go tell it on the moun - tain that Je - sus Christ is born.
rit.

GOD IS WITH US

Words and Music by
WAYNE KIRKPATRICK

© 2004 WARNER-TAMERLANE PUBLISHING CORP. and SELL THE COW MUSIC
All Rights Administered by WARNER-TAMERLANE PUBLISHING CORP.
All Rights Reserved

C♯m
Amaj9
F♯m7(4)
deep with-in I feel my soul is stir - ring as though my hope has
Verse 2:
Bsus
B
E2
B/E
E6/9
B/E
A(9)
been re-stored. 2. The shep-herds say they've heard the voice of an - gels, con-
E2
B/E
E6/9
B/E
A(9)
C♯m
firm - ing ru - mors spread a - cross the land that a Child, pro-tect - ed well from Her-od's
A
A6
F♯m7(4)
Bsus
an - ger, is our Fa-ther's Son, and the Son of man. Love is

Chorus:
C♯m
B/A
A
B/C♯
C♯m
B/C♯
A
rain - ing down on the world to - night; there's a pres-ence here, I can tell. God is
mf
D
E/D
E/A
A
F♯m
E
in us, God is for us, God is with us, Em - man - u - el. He's the
B/C♯
C♯m
B/C♯
B/A
A
B/C♯
C♯m
B/C♯
A2
Sav - ior we have been pray - ing for, in our hum - ble hearts He will dwell. God is
D
E/D
E/A
A
F♯m9
E
in us, God is for us, God is with us, Em - man - u - el.

D
E/A
A
F♯m7
3. I
mp
Verse 3:
E2
B/E
E6/9
B/E
A2
feel com - pelled to tell all who will lis - ten, that
E2
B/E
E6/9
B/E
A2
peace on earth is not so out of reach if we can
C♯m
A
find grace and mer - cy and for - give - ness. He has

Chorus:
F♯m7(4)
Bsus
B
C♯sus2 sus4
C♯m
come to save, He is all of these. Love is rain - ing down on the
mf
A2
A
C♯sus2 sus4
C♯m
C♯m7
A
world to - night; there's a pres - ence here, I can tell. God is
D
A
F♯m7(4)
E
in us, God is for us, God is with us, Em - man - u - el. He's the
C♯sus2 sus4
C♯m
A2
A
C♯sus2 sus4
C♯m
C♯m7
A
Sav - ior we have been pray-ing for, in our hum - ble hearts He will dwell. God is

To Coda
D
E/D
E/A
A
F♯m
E
in____ us, God is for____ us, God is with us, Em - man - u - el.
F♯m/C♯
C♯m7
A2
A
F♯m/C♯
C♯m7
A
Dmaj7
A
f
F♯m
F♯m7
E
F♯m/C♯
C♯
F♯sus2 sus4
F♯m
F♯m/C♯
C♯m7
F♯sus2 sus4
F♯m
Dmaj7
E/A
A
F♯m
F♯m7
E
D.S. 𝄋 al Coda
Love is

Coda
F♯m
with us.
You're the
dim.
8va
loco
p
A little slower
C♯m
C♯sus2
C♯sus4
Emaj7/B
A2
Sav - ior we have been pray - ing for, in our hum - ble hearts You will dwell. You are
D2
Amaj9
in us,
You are for us,
somewhat freely
8va
loco
Slowly
F♯m7(4)
B7sus
E
You are with us,
Em - man - u - el.

GROWN-UP CHRISTMAS LIST

Words and Music by
DAVID FOSTER and
LINDA THOMPSON JENNER

© 1990 WARNER-TAMERLANE PUBLISHING CORP., LINDA'S BOYS MUSIC and AIR BEAR MUSIC
All Rights on behalf of itself and LINDA'S BOYS MUSIC Administered by WARNER-TAMERLANE PUBLISHING CORP.
All Rights Reserved

B♭m7
Fm/A♭
G♭
D♭/F
E♭m7
6fr.
you still help some - how? I'm not a child_ but my heart still can
A♭7sus4
4fr.
A♭
4fr.
D♭
4fr.
A♭
4fr.
B♭m
dream. So here's my life long wish, my
B♭m7
Fm/A♭
G♭
D♭/F
E♭m7
6fr.
grown - up Christ - mas list, not for my - self— but for a world_ in
A♭7sus4
4fr.
A♭
4fr.
B♭
Gm7
3fr.
need. No more lives— torn a - part,_
rall.
a tempo
f

E♭maj7 Cm7 F7sus4 Dm7 Gm7 F6 E♭maj7 E♭/F F7
and wars would nev - er start, and time would heal— all hearts.
B♭ Gm7 E♭maj7 Cm7 F7sus4 Dm7 Gm7 F6
Ev - 'ry man would have— a friend,— that right would al - ways win, and love would nev - er
Em7-5 A13-9 E♭7 Dm7 Gm7 Cm7 F7sus4 B♭
end. This is my grown - up Christ - mas list.
rall.
a tempo
mp
Rubato
Fm7 B♭7sus4 B♭7 E♭ Gm7 C7sus4 C7
What is this il - lu - sion called, the in - no - cence of youth. May - be on - ly in our blind be - lief can we

F
A7sus4
A7
D
A
Bm
A
G
ev - er find the truth.
Oo.-
rall.
a tempo
D/F♯
Em7
A7sus4
A7
B
G♯m7
4fr.
There'd be
no more lives
torn a - part,-
rall.
a tempo
f
Emaj7
C♯7
4fr.
F♯7
D♯m7
6fr.
G♯m7
4fr.
F♯6
Emaj7
E/F♯
F♯7
and wars would nev-er start,
and time would heal
all hearts.
B
G♯m7
4fr.
Emaj7
C♯m7
4fr.
F♯7sus4
Ev - 'ry man would have
a friend,
and right would al - ways

D♯m7 6fr.
G♯m7 4fr.
F♯6
Fm7-5
B♭13-9 6fr.
E7
win, and love would nev - er end.
rall.
D♯m7 6fr.
G♯m7 4fr.
C♯m7 4fr.
F♯7
D♯m7 6fr.
G♯m7 4fr.
Fm7-5
E7
This is my grown-up Christ-mas list. This is my on - ly life - long—
a tempo
mp
rall.
D♯m7 6fr.
G♯m7 4fr.
C♯m7 4fr.
F♯7sus4
B
F♯
G♯m 4fr.
wish. This is my grown - up— Christ - mas list.
a tempo
rall.
a tempo
rall.
G♯m7 4fr.
D♯m7 6fr.
Emaj7
F♯7
B

HALLELUJAH! CHORUS

(from *The Messiah*)

By GEORGE FRIDERIC HANDEL

© 2009 ALFRED MUSIC PUBLISHING CO., INC.
All Rights Reserved

mf
lu - jah! Hal - le - lu - jah! Hal - le - lu - jah! For the Lord
mf
f
God om - ni - po - tent reign - eth. Hal-le - lu - jah! Hal - le - lu - jah! Hal - le -
f
f
f
mf
lu - jah! Hal - le - lu - jah! For the Lord God om - ni - po - tent
mf
f
f
reign - eth. Hal-le - lu - jah! Hal-le - lu - jah! Hal-le - lu - jah! Hal-le - lu - jah!
f

mf
For the Lord God om - ni - po-tent reign - eth.
mf
For the Lord God om - ni - po - tent reign - eth. Hal-le-lu-jah!
Hal-le-lu-jah! Hal-le-lu-jah! For the Lord God om - ni - po - tent
f
p
reign - eth Hal - le - lu - jah! The
f
p

mf
f
king - dom of this world is be - come the
mp
mf
f
king - dom of our Lord, and of His Christ, and of His Christ. And He shall
mf
reign for - ev - er and ev - er. And He shall reign for - ev - er and ev -
er. And He shall reign for - ev - er and ev - er. And

f
He shall reign for - ev - er and ev - er. King of
f
Kings, for - ev - er and ev - er. Hal - le - lu - jah! Hal - le - lu - jah! and Lord of
Lords. For - ev - er and ev - er. Hal - le - lu - jah! Hal - le - lu - jah! King of
Kings. For - ev - er and ev - er. Hal - le - lu - jah! Hal - le - lu - jah! And Lord of

ff
Lords. For - ev - er and ev - er. Hal-le-lu-jah! Hal-le - lu-jah! King of
Kings. For - ev - er and ev - er. Hal-le-lu-jah! Hal-le - lu - jah! And Lord of
mf
Lords. King of Kings and Lord of Lords. And He shall
mf
reign, and He shall reign. And He shall reign for -

f
ev - er and ev - er. King of Kings, for - ev - er and
f
ev - er, and Lord of Lords. Hal-le - lu - jah! Hal-le - lu - jah! And He shall
reign for - ev - er, for - ev - er and ev - er. King of
Kings and Lord of Lords. King of Kings and Lord of

Lords. And He shall reign for -
ev - er and ev - er. King of Kings and Lord of
Lords. Hal - le - lu - jah! Hal - le - lu - jah! Hal - le - lu - jah! Hal - le -
Largo
ff
lu - jah! Hal - le - lu - jah!
ff

HARK! THE HERALD ANGELS SING

Words by
CHARLES WESLEY

Music by
FELIX MENDELSSOHN

© 2009 ALFRED MUSIC PUBLISHING CO., INC.
All Rights Reserved

Am G/B C F G7 C N.C. F C7 F C
God and sin - ners rec - on - ciled." Joy - ful, all ye na - tions, rise,
off - spring of a vir - gin's womb. Veiled in flesh, the God - head, see.
ris'n with heal - ing in His wings. Mild he lays His glo - ry by,
N.C. F C7 F C B♭ F Gm D Gm
join the tri - umph of the skies. With an - gel - ic host pro - claim,
Hail the in - car - nate De - i - ty. Pleased as man, with man to dwell,
born that man no more may die. Born to raise the sons of earth,
C F F/C C7 F B♭ F Gm D Gm
"Christ is born in Beth - le - hem."
Je - sus our Em - man - u - el!
born to give them sec - ond birth.
Hark! The her - ald an - gels sing,
f
C F 1.2. F/C C7 F 3. F/C C7 F
"Glo - ry to the new - born King." new - born King."

HERE WE COME A-CAROLING

(The Wassail Song)

Old English

© 2009 ALFRED MUSIC PUBLISHING CO., INC.
All Rights Reserved

B♭7 E♭ B♭ C7 Fm7 E♭/B♭ B♭7
too. And God bless you and send you a
E♭ Cm Fm7 E♭ A♭ B♭ C7
Hap - py New Year. And God send you a
1.2. 3.
(𝅗𝅥 = ♩.)
Fm7 E♭/B♭ B♭ E♭ E♭
Hap - py New Year. 2. We Year.
3. God

HAVE YOURSELF A MERRY LITTLE CHRISTMAS

Words and Music by
HUGH MARTIN and RALPH BLANE

© 1943 (Renewed) METRO-GOLDWYN-MAYER INC.
© 1944 (Renewed) EMI FEIST CATALOG INC.
All Rights Controlled by EMI FEIST CATALOG INC. (Publishing) and ALFRED MUSIC PUBLISHING CO., INC. (Print)
All Rights Reserved

Dm7 F/G G7 C Am G11 G7
mer - ry lit - tle Christ - mas; make the Yule - tide gay.
C Am Dm7 E7 Am Gm7 C7 C+
From now on, our trou - bles will be miles a - way.
F Fm C/E E♭dim7 Dm7 F/G G+
Here we are as in old - en days, hap - py gold - en days of
Cmaj7 F♯m7(♭5) B7(♯5) B7 Em G+
yore. Faith - ful friends who are dear to us gath - er

G/D Am D7 F/G G7 C Am7 Dm7 F/G G7
near to us once more. Through the years we all will be to - geth - er,
C Am G11 G7 C Am Dm7 E7
if the Fates al - low. Hang a shin - ing star up - on the high - est
Am C+ F Am
bough, and have your - self a
Dm7 G7(♭9) C Cmaj9 Am Cmaj7
mer - ry lit - tle Christ - mas now.
rit.

(There's No Place Like)

HOME FOR THE HOLIDAYS

Words by
AL STILLMAN

Music by
ROBERT ALLEN

© 1954 (Renewed) RONCOM MUSIC CO.
Copyright Assigned to CHARLIE DEITCHER PRODUCTIONS INC. and MUSIC SALES CORPORATION
All Rights Reserved

C
E♭dim7
G7
Dm7
To Coda
friend - ly gaze,
mil - lion ways,
for the hol - i - days you
G7
C
F
C
B♭/C
C7
can't beat home, sweet home.
I met a
F
F♯dim7
man who lives in Ten - nes - see, and he was head - in'
C
C♯dim7
G7
F♯7
G7
for Penn - syl - va - nia and some home - made pump - kin

C
C7
B♭/C
C7
F
pie.
From Penn - syl - va - nia, folks are
F♯dim7
C
Cm
trav - 'lin' down to Dix - ie's sun - ny shore.
From At -
D.S. 𝄋 al Coda
G
G♯dim7
Am7
D7
G7
C♯dim7
Dm7
G7
lan - tic to Pa - cif - ic, gee, the traf - fic is ter - rif - ic. Oh, there's
Coda
G7
C♯dim7
Dm7
G9
G7(♭9)
C
F/G
C
can't beat home, sweet home.
cresc.
f

I WANT AN OLD-FASHIONED CHRISTMAS

Words by
FLORENCE TARR

Music by
FAY FOSTER

© 1945 (Renewed) EMI ROBBINS CATALOG INC.
All Rights Controlled by EMI ROBBINS CATALOG INC. (Publishing) and ALFRED MUSIC PUBLISHING CO., INC. (Print)
All Rights Reserved

C7
F
G♯dim7
Gm7
C7
want an old - fash - ioned Christ - mas, to feel the soft cold___
F
G♯dim7
C/G
G7
C
Am
Dm7
snow, and home - folks cheer - i - ly nod - ding a mer - ry
C/G
G7
C
warm___ "Hel - lo!"
E♭7
A♭
B♭m7
I want to hear the lit - tle

D♭
A♭
D♭
D♭m
A♭
A♭6
D7(♭5)
chil - dren sing - ing the Christ - mas car - ols I used to know; and
C/G
G7
C/G
G7
Am7
hear the eve - ning church bells ring - ing out their joy - ous wel - come of
Dm7
G7
C
Dm
E7
long a - go.
I
rit.
C
G7
C
want an old - fash - ioned Christ - mas, to be a child a -
a tempo

C7
F
G7
C
A7
gain, to make be - lieve that there's a San - ta,
Dm7(♭5)
G7
C
G7
C
G7
for I was hap - pi - est then. Mer - ry Christ-mas! Mer - ry
F+
A7
Dm7
C
Christ - mas! Mer - ry Christ - mas!
a tempo
rit.

I'LL BE HOME FOR CHRISTMAS

Words by
KIM GANNON

Music by
WALTER KENT

© 1943 (Renewed) GANNON & KENT MUSIC CO., INC.
All Rights Reserved

Refrain:
C
Cdim7
Dm7
G7
Dm7
G7
I'll be home for Christ - mas.
p–mf
C6
Em7(♭5)
A7
Dm
Em7(♭5)
F6
Gm
G♯dim7
A7
You can plan on me.
r.h.
Dm
Dm7(♭5)
G7
C
G/B
Am
Please have snow and mis - tle - toe and
Am7
D7
Am
D7(♭9)
G9
C♯dim7
Dm7
G6
pres - ents on the tree.

120
C6
Cdim7
Dm7
G7
Dm7
G7
Christ - mas Eve will find me
C6
Em7(♭5)
A7
Dm7
F6
where the love - light gleams.
I'll be
Fm6
C/G
Em7(♭5)
A7
Dm
Dm7
G7
home for Christ - mas, if on - ly in my
mf
1.
C
G7(♭9)
2.
C
C♯dim7
G7(♭9)
C
dreams.
dreams.
rit.
mp

IT'S THE MOST WONDERFUL TIME OF THE YEAR

Words and Music by
EDDIE POLA and GEORGE WYLE

© 1963 (Renewed) BARNABY MUSIC CORP.
All Rights Reserved

1.
2.
Fm7 B♭7 G♭ Fm7 B♭7 B♭m7
time of the year. It's the
sea - son of all.
E♭7 B♭m7 E♭7 A♭ A♭dim E♭/B♭ Cm7
There'll be par-ties for host-ing, marsh-mal-lows for toast-ing and
Fm7 B♭7 E♭ E♭7 A♭m7 D♭7
car - ol - ing out in the snow. There'll be scar - y ghost sto - ries and
G♭maj7 E♭m Fm7(♭5) C♭7 Fm7/B♭ B♭7 Fm7
tales of the glo-ries of Christ-mas-es long long a - go.

B♭9 E♭ Cm Fm7 B♭7 E♭ Cm
It's the most won-der-ful time of the year.
Fm7 B♭7 Fm7 B♭7 E♭ E♭7
There'll be much mis-tle-toe-ing and hearts will be glow-ing, when
A♭ A♭dim E♭
loved ones are near. It's the most
Cm7 Fm7 B♭7 E♭ C♭ A♭m E♭
won-der-ful time of the year.

JINGLE BELL ROCK

Words and Music by
JOE BEAL and JIM BOOTHE

© 1957 (Renewed) CHAPPELL & CO., INC.
All Rights Reserved

Dm7
G7
G7(♯5)
C
now the Jin - gle - hop has be - gun.
Jin - gle - bell, Jin - gle - bell,
C♯dim7
Dm7
G7
Jin - gle - bell rock.
Jin - gle - bells chime in jin - gle - bell time.
Dm7
G7
Dm7
G7
D7
G7
C
Dm
C7
Danc - in' and pranc - in' in Jin - gle - bell Square in the frost - y air.
What a
F
F♯dim7
C
bright time, it's the right time to rock the night a - way.
Jin - gle -

Am7 D7 Am7 D7 G7 Dm7 G7
bell time is a swell time to go glid-in' in a one-horse sleigh.
C Em7(♭5) A7(♯5)
Gid-dy-yap, jin-gle horse, pick up your feet. Jin-gle a-round the clock.
F Fm6 D7 G7 1. C C♯dim7 Dm7 G7
Mix and min-gle in a jin-gl-in' beat, that's the Jin-gle-bell rock.
2. D7 G7 D7 G7 F C Dm7 B C
that's the Jin-gle-bell, that's the Jin-gle-bell rock.

JINGLE BELLS

Words and Music by
JAMES PIERPONT

© 2009 ALFRED MUSIC PUBLISHING CO., INC.
All Rights Reserved

G
way. Bells on bob - tail ring
side. The horse was lean and lank; mis -
song. Just get a bob - tailed nag, two -
C
Am
mak - ing spir - its bright; what fun it is to
for - tune seemed his lot. He got in - to a
for - ty for his speed, then hitch him to an
G/D
D7
G
D7
ride and sing a sleigh - ing song to - night.
drift - ed bank and whew, we got up - set!
o - pen sleigh and crack, you'll take the lead!
Oh!
Chorus:
G
Jin - gle bells, jin - gle bells, jin - gle all the

C
G
way. Oh, what fun it is to ride in a
A7
D7
G
one - horse o - pen sleigh! Jin - gle bells,
C
jin - gle bells, jin - gle all the way. Oh, what fun it
G
D7
1.2.
G
3.
G
is to ride in a one - horse o - pen sleigh! 2. A sleigh!

JOY TO THE WORLD

Words by
ISAAC WATTS

Music by
GEORGE F. HANDEL

© 2009 ALFRED MUSIC PUBLISHING CO., INC.
All Rights Reserved

room, and heav'n and na - ture sing, and
plains re - peat the sound - ing joy, re -
ness and won - ders of His love, and
p
mp
A
A7
D
G
heav'n and na - ture sing, and heav'n and
peat the sound - ing joy, re - peat, re -
won - ders of His love, and won - ders,
mf
D
Em
D/A
A7
1.2.
D
3.
D
heav'n and na - ture sing. love.
peat the sound - ing joy.
won - ders of His

LAST CHRISTMAS

Words and Music by
GEORGE MICHAEL

© 1984 WHAM MUSIC LIMITED
All Rights Administered by WARNER/CHAPPELL MUSIC INTERNATIONAL LTD.
All Rights Reserved

Chorus:
Dmaj9
D6
Dmaj9
D6
F♯m7/B
Bm7
Last Christ - mas I gave you my heart, but the ver - y next day you
F♯m7/B
Bm7
Bm7/E
Em7
Bm7/E
Em7
gave it a - way. This year to save me from tears I'll
To Coda
1.3.5.
2.4.
Gmaj7/A
A9
Gmaj7/A
A9
Gmaj7/A
A9
give it to some - one spe - cial.
cial.
Interlude:
Dmaj9
D6
Dmaj9
D6
F♯m7/B
Bm7
F♯m7/B
Bm7

134
Em9
Em7
Em9
Em
Gmaj7/A
A9
Gmaj7/A
A7
Verse 1 (sing 1st time only):
Dmaj9
D6
Dmaj9
D6
F♯m7/B
Bm7
1. Once bit - ten and twice shy, I keep my dis-tance but
Verse 2 (sing 2nd time only):
2. A crowd - ed room, friends with tired eyes, I'm hid - ing from you
F♯m7/B
Bm7
Bm7/E
Em7
Bm7/E
Em7
tears still catch my eye. Tell me, ba - by, do you rec - og - nize me?
and your soul of ice. My god, I thought you were some-one to re-ly on.

Gmaj7/A
A9
Gmaj7/A
A9
Dmaj9
D6
Well, it's been a year. It does-n't sur-prise_ me. Hap-py Christ-mas, I
Me, I guess I was a shoul-der to cry___ on. A face on a lov-er with a
Dmaj9
D6
F♯m7/B
Bm7
F♯m7/B
Bm7
wrapped it up and sent it with a note say-ing, "I_____ love you." I meant it.
fire in his heart,_ a man un-der-cov-er, but you tore me___ a-
Bm7/E
Em7
Bm7/E
Em7
Gmaj7/A
A9
Now_ I know_ what a fool_____ I've been._ But if you kissed me now,___ I know you'd
part._____ Ooo,_____ now I've found a real___ love. You'll nev-er

1.
D.S. 𝄋
2.
D.S. 𝄋 al Coda
(with repeat)
Gmaj7/A
A9
Gmaj7/A
A9
fool me a - gain.
fool me a - gain.
Coda
Gmaj7/A
A7
Dmaj9
D6
Dmaj9
D6
cial. A face on a lov - er with a fire in his heart, a
F♯m7/B
Bm7
F♯m7/B
Bm7
Bm7/E
Em7
man un - der - cov - er, but you tore him a - part.
May - be next year

Bm7/E
Em7
Gmaj7/A
A9
Gmaj7/A
A9
I'll give it to some - one, I'll give it to some - one spe -
Dmaj9
D6
Dmaj9
D6
F♯m7/B
Bm7
cial, spe - cial.
Some-one,
F♯m7/B
Bm7
Bm7/E
Em7
Bm7/E
Em7
some-one. I'll
Gmaj7/A
A9
Gmaj7/A
A9
Repeat and fade
give it to some - one, I'll give it to some - one spe -

LET IT SNOW! LET IT SNOW! LET IT SNOW!

Words by
SAMMY CAHN

Music by
JULE STYNE

© 1945 (Renewed) PRODUCERS MUSIC PUBL. CO., INC. and CAHN MUSIC CO.
All Rights on Behalf of PRODUCERS MUSIC PUBL. CO., INC. Administered by CHAPPELL & CO., INC.
All Rights Reserved

C7
F
F/A
A♭dim7
does - n't show signs of stop - ping, and I brought some corn for
C7
D7
Gm
D+
D7
Gm
A♭dim7
pop - ping. The lights are turned way down low. Let it
f
C7
F
C
snow, let it snow, let it snow! When we fi - nal - ly kiss good -
mf
C♯dim7
Dm7
G7
C
night, how I'll hate go - ing out in the storm! But if

B+
B♭6
A7
D7
G7
you real - ly hold me tight, all the way home I'll be
C
F/C
C7
F
C7
F
warm. The fi - re is slow - ly dy - ing, and, my
mf
F/A
A♭dim7
C7
D7
Gm
D+
D7
dear, we're still good - bye - ing. But as long as you love me
Gm
A♭dim7
C7
1.
F
2.
F
so, let it snow, let it snow, let it snow! Oh, the snow!
f
sfz

LET THERE BE PEACE ON EARTH

(Let It Begin With Me)

Words and Music by
SY MILLER and JILL JACKSON

© 1955 (Renewed) JAN-LEE MUSIC, Beverly Hills, CA
All Rights Reserved Used by Permission

Am Em C7 F G G7
God as our Fa - ther, {broth - ers / fam - 'ly} all are
mf
C Am D G
we. Let {me / us} walk with {my broth - er / each oth - er} in
Am7 D6 D G7 G C Am
per - fect har - mo - ny. Let peace be -
mp
Dm7 G7 C F C Dm7 G
gin with me; let this be the mo - ment now.

C
B
B7
Em
B
With ev - 'ry step I take, let this be my sol - emn
G(9)
G
C
C+
vow; to take each mo - ment and live each mo - ment in
cresc.
mf
cresc. poco a poco
F
Fdim
F
D7
Fm6
C
E7
peace e - ter - nal - ly! Let there be
f
F
C
F
G(9)
G7sus
C
peace on earth, and let it be - gin with me.
rit.

THE LITTLE DRUMMER BOY

Words and Music by
HARRY SIMEONE, HENRY ONORATI
and KATHERINE DAVIS

© 1958 (Renewed) EMI MILLS MUSIC, INC. and INTERNATIONAL KORWIN CORP.
Worldwide Print Rights Administered by ALFRED MUSIC PUBLISHING CO., INC.
All Rights Reserved

F
B♭
rum pum pum pum, to lay be - fore the king, pa -
rum pum pum pum, that's fit to give our King pa -
F7
B♭
F
C
rum pum pum pum, rum pum pum pum, rum pum pum pum.
rum pum pum pum, rum pum pum pum, rum pum pum pum.
F
So to hon - or Him, pa - rum pum pum pum,
Shall I play for you, pa - rum pum pum pum,
1.
C7
F
when we come.
f

2.
C7
F
C
on my drum?
f
l.h.
F
3. Mar - y nod - ded, pa - rum pum pum pum,
the ox and lamb kept time, pa - rum pum pum pum.
C
I played my drum for Him, pa - rum pum pum pum,

F
F7
B♭
F
I played my best for Him, pa - rum pum pum pum, rum pum pum pum,
C
F
C
rum pum pum pum.
r.h.
l.h.
Slower
F
Then He smiled at me, pa - rum pum pum pum,
C7
F
me and my drum.
f

THE LITTLE DRUMMER BOY/PEACE ON EARTH

PEACE ON EARTH:
Words by
ALAN KOHAN
Music by
LARRY GROSSMAN
and IAN FRASER

THE LITTLE DRUMMER BOY:
Words and Music by
HARRY SIMEONE, HENRY ONORATI
and KATHERINE DAVIS

PEACE ON EARTH:
© 1977 (Renewed) WARNER-TAMERLANE PUBLISHING CORP., PHRASER-MORTON MUSIC and ONE ZEE MUSIC
All Rights for PHRASER-MORTON MUSIC Administered by WB MUSIC CORP.
All Rights Reserved

THE LITTLE DRUMMER BOY:
© 1958 (Renewed) EMI MILLS MUSIC, INC. and INTERNATIONAL KORWIN CORP.
Worldwide Print Rights Administered by ALFRED MUSIC PUBLISHING CO., INC.
All Rights Reserved

B♭sus2 sus4
B♭
A new - born King to see, pa rum pum pum pum.
F7
B♭
B♭7
E♭/B♭
B♭
Our fin - est gifts we bring, pa rum pum pum pum, rum pum pum pum,
(♩ = 𝅗𝅥)
F
rum pum pum pum.
𝄋 Verse:
B♭
B♭sus
B♭
David:
1. Peace on earth, can it be?
2. I pray my wish will come true
Bing:
1. Come they told me, pa rum pum pum pum.
2.Lit - tle Ba - by, pa rum pum pum pum.

E♭/B♭
B♭
Years from now, per - haps we'll see,
for my child and your child too.
A new - born King to see, pa rum pum pum pum.
I stood be - side Him there, pa rum pum pum pum.
F
He'll see the
see the
day of glo - ry,
Our fin - est gifts we bring, pa rum pum pum pum.
I played my drum for him, pa rum pum pum pum.
cresc.
B♭
B♭7sus
E♭/B♭
B♭
see the day when men of good will live in
To lay be - fore the king, pa rum pum pum pum, rum pum pum pum,
I played my best for Him, pa rum pum pum pum, rum pum pum pum,

Fsus
F
F2
F
B♭
peace, live in peace a - gain. Peace on earth,
rum pum pum pum. So to hon - or Him, pa
rum pum pum pum. Then He smiled at me, pa
decresc.
B♭sus
B♭
B♭sus2 sus4
To Coda
B♭
can it be?
rum pum pum pum, when we come.
rum pum pum pum, me and my
cresc.
Bridge:
Fm7
B♭7
E♭maj7
Cm7
Both:
Ev - 'ry child must be made a - ware.
mf
Fm7
B♭7
E♭maj7
Cm7
Ev - 'ry child must be made to care,

152
E♭m7
A♭7
D♭maj7
B♭m7
care e - nough for his fel - low man to
Cm7(♭5)
F7sus
F7
D.S. 𝄋 al Coda
give all the love that he can.
decresc.
Coda
B♭
E♭/B♭
B♭
be?
drum.
decresc.
B♭sus2 sus4
B♭
E♭/B♭
B♭
Both:
Can it be?
rit.

THESE ARE THE SPECIAL TIMES

Words and Music by
DIANE WARREN

© 1998 REALSONGS (ASCAP)
All Rights Reserved

F♯
B♭7
D♯m7
You and I sharing this time together,
you and I travel through time together,
G♯m7
E
sharing the same dream. As time goes by,
living this sweet dream. And ev'ry day,
Chorus:
G♯m7/C♯
F♯
we will find
we can say
these are the special times, times we'll re-
B/F♯
G♯m7
F♯/A♯
member. These are the precious times, the tender times we'll

C♯
F♯
hold in our hearts for - ev - er. These are the sweet - est times, these times to -
B♭7sus
B♭7
D♯m7
B♭7/D
F♯/C♯
geth - er. And through it all, one thing will al - ways be true,
Bm6
G♯m7
G♯m7/C♯
the spe - cial times are the times I share, with
1.
Emaj9
you.
2.
Emaj9
you.

Bridge:
B
F♯/A♯
G♯m7
D♯m7
These ten - der mo - ments, when heav - en is so close,
Amaj9
G♯m7
G♯m7/C♯
Am7/D
these are the mo - ments that I know. These are the
Chorus:
G
C/G
spe - cial times, times we'll re - mem - ber. These are the
Am7
G/B
D
pre - cious times, the ten - der times we'll hold in our hearts for - ev - er. These are the

G
B7sus
B7
sweet - est times, these times to - geth - er. And through it
Em7
B7/D♯
G/D
Cm6
Am7
Am7/D
all, one thing will al - ways be true, the spe-cial times are the times I share, the
Bm7
Em7
Am7
Am7/D
D
spe - cial times are the times we share, the spe - cial times are the times I share
Fmaj9
G(9)
with you.

THE MARVELOUS TOY

© 1961 (Renewed) FSMGI (IMRO) and CHERRY LANE MUSIC PUBLISHING CO., INC. (ASCAP)
All Rights for FSMGI (IMRO) Administered by STATE ONE SONGS AMERICA (ASCAP)
All Rights Reserved

Verse 2:
The first time that I picked it up, I had a big surprise,
For right on its bottom were two big buttons that looked like big green eyes.
I first pushed one and then the other, and then I twisted its lid,
And when I set it down again, here is what it did:
(To Chorus 2:)

Verse 3:
It first marched left and then marched right and then marched under a chair,
And when I looked where it had gone, it wasn't even there!
I started to sob and my daddy laughed, for he knew that I would find
When I turned around my marvelous toy, chugging from behind.
(To Chorus 3:)

Verse 4:
Well, the years have gone by too quickly, it seems, and I have my own little boy.
And yesterday I gave him my marvelous little toy.
His eyes nearly popped right out of his head, and he gave a squeal of glee.
Neither one of us knows just what it is, but he loves it, just like me.
(To Chorus 4:)

Chorus 4:
It still goes "zip" when it moves, and "bop" when it stops,
And "whirr" when it stands still.
I never knew just what it was
And I guess I never will.

MARY, DID YOU KNOW?

Words and Music by
MARK LOWRY and
BUDDY GREENE

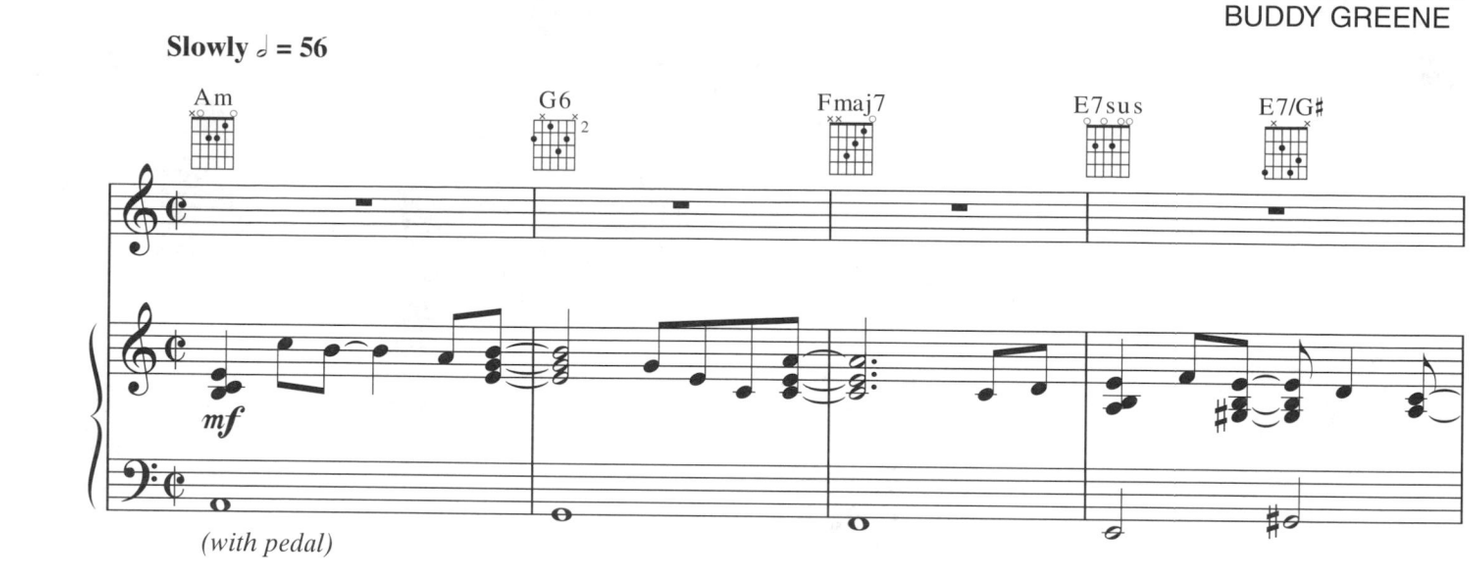

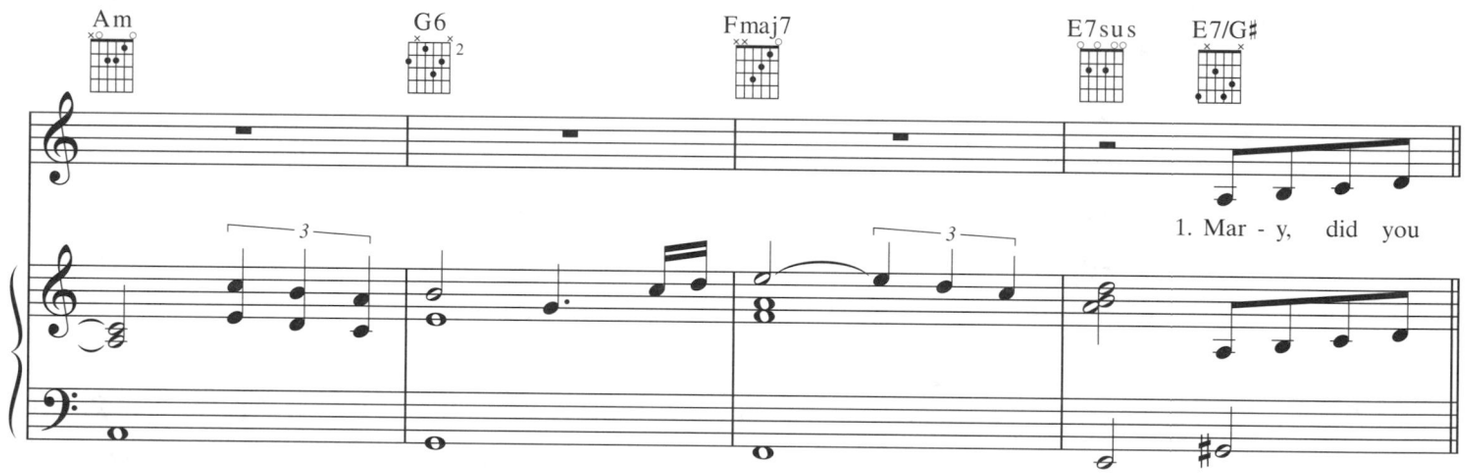

𝄋 *Verse:*

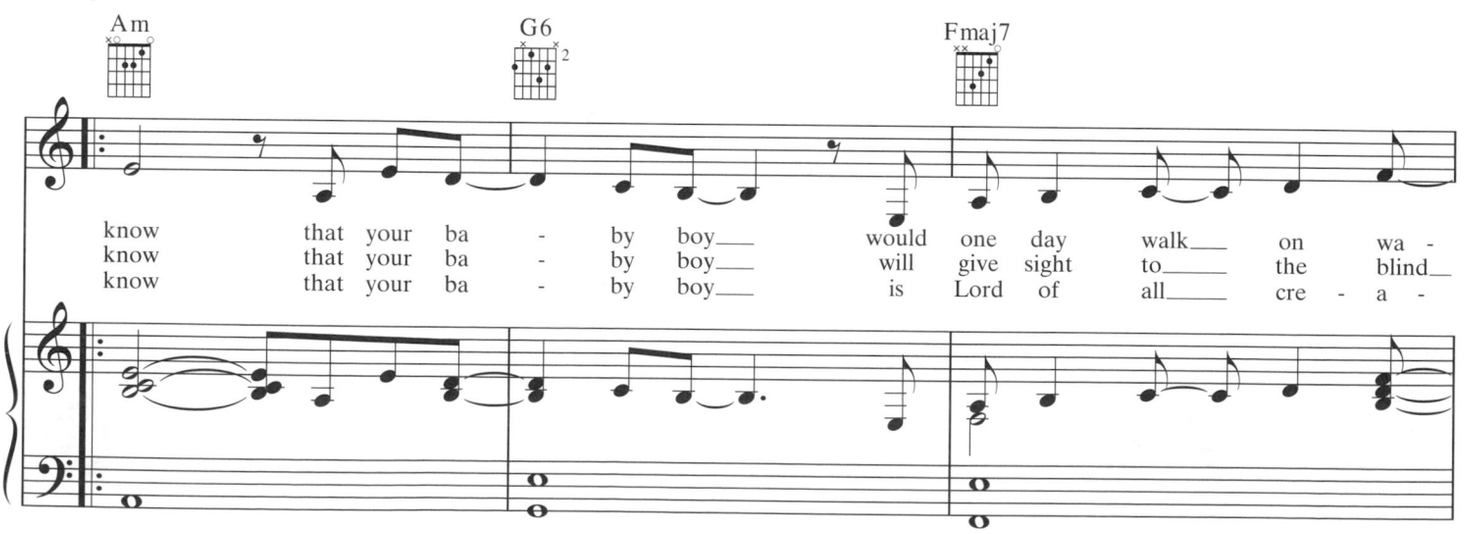

© 1991 WORD MUSIC, INC. and RUFUS MUSIC
All Rights Reserved Used by Permission

E7sus
E7/G♯
Am
G6
ter? Mar - y, did you know that your ba - by boy would
man? Mar - y, did you know that your ba - by boy would
tion? Mar - y, did you know that your ba - by boy will
Fmaj7
E7sus
E7/G♯
F
save our sons and daugh - ters? Did you know that your ba -
calm a storm with his hand? Did you know that your ba -
one day rule the na - tions? Did you know that your ba -
G/F
C
G/B
by boy has come to make you new?
by boy has walked where an - gels trod,
by boy was heav - en's per - fect lamb,
Am
Fmaj7
This child that you de - liv -
that when you kiss your lit - tle ba -
and the sleep - ing child you're hold -

To Coda
E7sus
1.
E7/G♯
ered will soon de - liv - er you? 2. Mar - y, did you
by, you've kissed the face of God?
ing is the
2.
E7/G♯
Am
G6
Fmaj7
E7sus
E7/G♯
Am
G6
Fmaj7
E7sus
E7/G♯
The
Bridge:
F
G
Am
blind will see, the deaf will hear, the dead will live a - gain.

Fmaj7
Dm7
E7sus
E7
The lame will leap, the dumb will speak the
Am
E7
D.S. 𝄋 al Coda
prais - es of the lamb. 3. Mar - y, did you
Coda
E7sus
E7/G♯
Am
great
I
Am?
know?
Repeat ad lib. and fade
G6
Fmaj7
E7sus
E7/G♯
Mar - y, did you

NATIVITY CAROL

Words and Music by
JOHN RUTTER

Andante tranquillo ♩ = 108

D Bm G

p

D G/D D Bm G/B F♯m/A

1. Born in a sta - ble so bare, Born so
2. Cra - dled by moth - er so fair, Ten - der her
3. Wise men from dis - tant far land, Shep - herds from
4. Love in that sta - ble was born In - to our

p – mp

G6 A9/C♯ G/D D Bm7 D/A G/D A7/E

long a - go. Born 'neath light of
lul - la - by. O - ver her Son so
star - ry hills Wor - ship this babe so
hearts to flow. In - no - cent dream - ing

F♯m7 G/D G A7 Dsus D

star He who loved us so.
dear An - gel hosts fill the sky.
rare. Hearts with His warmth He fills.
babe, Make me thy love to know.

© 1967 (Renewed) OXFORD UNIVERSITY PRESS
All Rights Reserved Used by Permission

G/B A7sus A7 F♯m Bm F♯m/A G
Far a - way, si - lent He lay, Born to -
pp cresc. poco a poco
F♯m Bm E7 Asus A Dmaj7 Em/D Dmaj7 A9
day, your hom - age pay; For Christ is born for
f
1.3.
F♯m7 Bm Em7 F♯+ Em/G A7 D G/D A7sus A7
aye, Born on Christ - mas Day.
dim.
mp
2.
Em/G A D
Christ - mas Day.
4.
Em/G A7 D
Christ - mas Day.
rit. e dim.
pp

O CHRISTMAS TREE

(O Tannenbaum)

TRADITIONAL

© 2009 ALFRED MUSIC PUBLISHING CO., INC.
All Rights Reserved

Gm C7 F D
stand in ver - dant beau - ty! Your boughs are green in
rich - ly God has decked thee! Thou bidst us true and
treu sind dei - ne Blät - ter. Du grünst - nicht nur zur
Gm C7 Fsus F C
sum - mer's glow, and do not fade in win - ter's snow. O Christ - mas tree, O
faith - ful be, and trust in God un - chang - ing - ly. O Christ - mas tree, O
som - mer - zeit, nein auch im win - ter wenn es schneit. O Tan - nen - baum, O
F D Gm C7 1. Fsus F 2. Fsus F
Christ - mas tree, you stand in ver - dant beau - ty. 2. O decked thee!
Christ - mas tree, how rich - ly God has O Blät - ter.
Tan - nen - baum, wie treu sind dei - ne

O HOLY NIGHT

(Cantique de Noël)

Words and Music by
J. S. DWIGHT and ADOLPHE ADAM

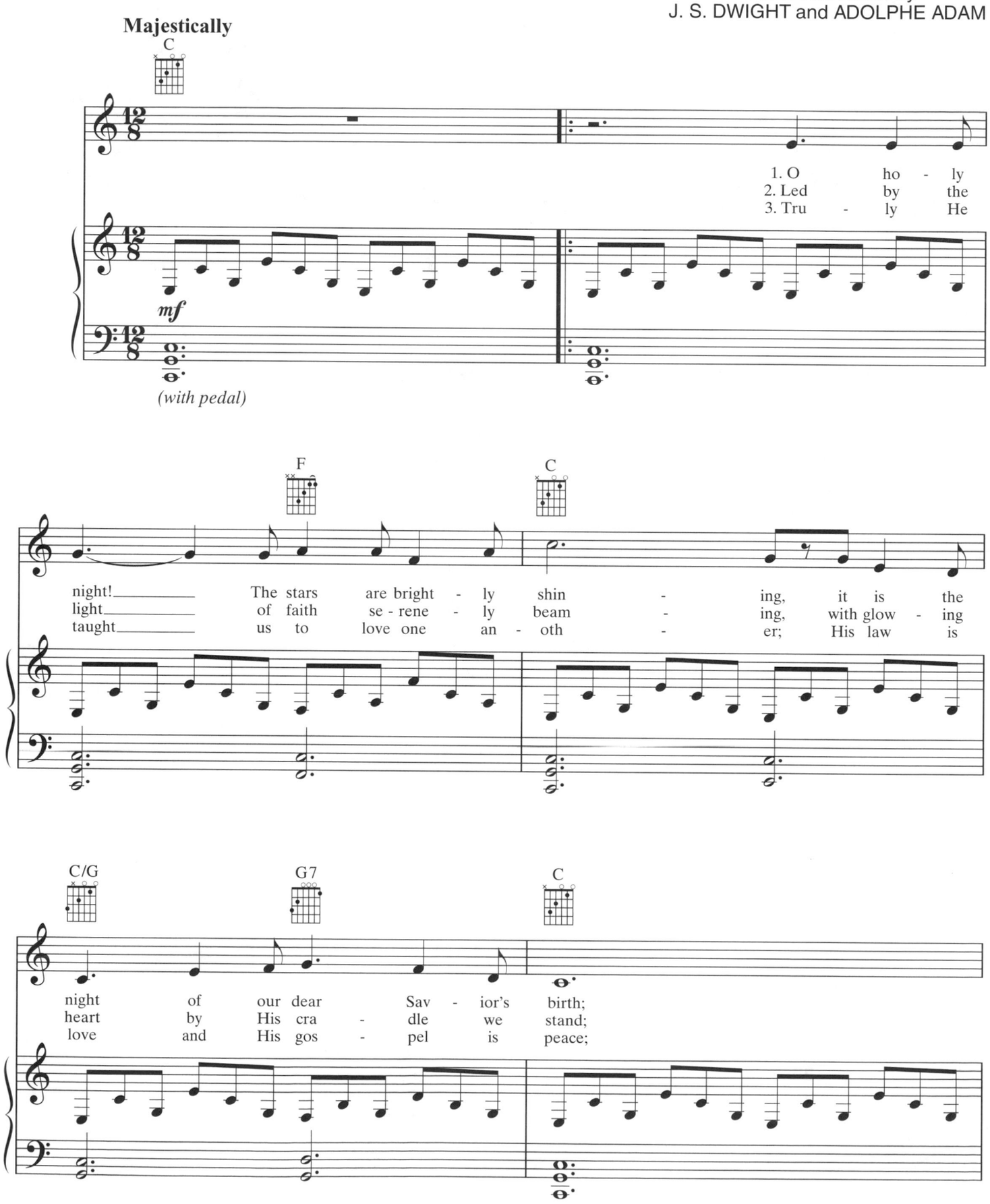

© 2009 ALFRED MUSIC PUBLISHING CO., INC.
All Rights Reserved

F
long lay the world in sin and sor - row
so led by light of a star sweet - ly
Chains shall He break, for the slave is our
C
C7
Em
B7
pin - ing, till He ap - peared and the soul felt its
gleam - ing, here came the wise men from the O - rient
broth - er, and in His name all op - pres - sion shall
Em
G7
worth. A thrill of hope, the
land. The King of kings lay
cease. With hymns of joy in
C
G7
wea - ry world re - joic - es, for yon - der breaks a
thus in low - ly man - ger, in all our tri - als
grate - ful cho - rus rais - ing, let ev - 'ry heart a -

C
Am
new and glo - rious morn! Fall on your
born to be our friend; He knows our
dore His Ho - ly Name! Christ is the
cresc.
f
Em
Dm
knees! O hear the an - gel
need, He guard - eth us from
Lord! With saint and ser - aph
Am
C/G
G7
C
F
voic - es! O night di - vine! O
dan - ger, be - hold your King! Be -
prais - ing, His pow'r and glo - ry
C
G7
C
G
G7/F
night when Christ was born! O night di -
fore the low - ly bend! Be - hold your
ev - er - more pro - claim! His pow'r and

C/E
F6
C/G
G7
vine! O night, O night di -
King! Be - fore the low - ly
glo - ry ev - er - more pro -
1.2.
C
3.
C
vine!
bend!
claim!
F
Dm
G7
C
F6
C/G
G7
C

O LITTLE TOWN OF BETHLEHEM

Words by
PHILLIPS BROOKS

Music by
LEWIS H. REDNER

© 2009 ALFRED MUSIC PUBLISHING CO., INC.
All Rights Reserved

Gm6
G♯dim7
A
N.C.
Gm
in the dark streets shin - eth the ev - er - last - ing
morn - ing stars to - geth - er pro - claim the ho - ly
ear may hear His com - ing, but in this world of
hear the Christ - mas an - gels the great glad tid - ings
A
F
B♭
Light; the hopes and fears of all the years are
birth! And prais - es sing to God the King, and
sin, where meek souls will re - ceive Him, still the
tell; O come to us, a - bide with us, our
1.2.3.
4.
F/C
G7
F/C
C7
F
F
met in thee to - night.
peace to all on earth.
dear Christ en - ters in.
Lord Em - man - u -
2. For
3. How
4. O
el!

THE PRAYER

Italian Lyric by
ALBERTO TESTA and TONY RENIS

Words and Music by
CAROLE BAYER SAGER and DAVID FOSTER

© 1996 WARNER-TAMERLANE PUBLISHING CORP. and WB MUSIC CORP.
All Rights Reserved

F/A
B♭
Gm/C
and help us to be wise
in times when we don't
E♭/F
F
poco rit.
know.
Let this be our
poco rit.
Chorus:
Gm
a tempo
Gm7/C
C7
A7sus
prayer,
when we lose our
way.
a tempo
A7
Dm
B♭
Dm
Am
Lead us to a place,
guide us with your grace

B♭
F/C
C
B♭/F
F
to a place where we'll be safe.
Male:
mf
La lu - ce che tu
mf
Verse 2:
B♭
mf
C7sus
C7
F
I pray we'll find your light,
and hold it in our
dai,
nel cuo - re res - te - rá.
F/A
B♭
Csus
C
Gm/C
C
hearts
when stars go out each night,
A ri - cor - dar - ci che
l'e - ter - na ste - lla

E♭/F
F7
poco rit.
oh.
cresc.
poco rit.
sei.
Ne - lla mia pre -
cresc.
poco rit.
Chorus:
a tempo
Gm
Gm7/C
C7
A7sus
Let this be our prayer,
when shad - ows fill our
a tempo
ghie - ra
quan - ta fe - de c'é.
a tempo
f
A7
Dm
B♭
Dm
Am
mp
day.
guide us with your grace.
mp
Lead us to a place,
dim.
mp

B♭ F/C C7 B♭/F F
cresc.
Give us faith so we'll be safe. So - gna - mo un
cresc.
Give us faith so we'll be safe. So - gna - mo un
cresc.
Bridge:
C/B♭ B♭ C/B♭ Fsus F C/B♭ B♭ C/B♭
mf
mon - do sen - za piú vio - len - za. Un mon - do di giu - sti - zia e di spe -
mf
mon - do sen - za piú vio - len - za. Un mon - do di giu - sti - zia e di spe -
mf
Fsus F B♭maj7 Fsus F Dm
ran - za. O - gnu - no dia la ma - no al suo vi - ci - no sim - bo - lo di
ran - za. O - gnu - no dia la ma - no al suo vi - ci - no sim - bo - lo di

D♭ B♭m Fsus F
cresc.
pa - ce, di tra - ter - ni - tá.
pa - ce, di tra - ter - ni - tá.
La for - za che ci
Verse 3:
E♭ Fsus F Fsus F B♭
f
We ask that life be kind,
and watch us from a -
dai
é il de - si - de - rio che.
B♭(9)/D E♭ Fsus F
bove.
We hope each soul will find
O - gnu - no tro - vi a - more
in - tor - no e den - tro

A♭/B♭
B♭
mf
an - oth - er soul to love. Let this be our
sé. Let this be our
dim.
Chorus:
Cm
Cm7/F
F7
F7/E♭
D7sus
prayer, let this be our prayer, just like ev - 'ry
prayer, just like ev - 'ry child,
mf
D7
Gm
E♭
Gm
Dm
mp
child, need to find a place, guide us with your grace.
need to find a place, guide us with your grace.
dim.
mp

E♭
B♭/F
F7
E♭/B♭
B♭
B♭/A
cresc.
Give us faith so we'll be safe.
Freely
Gm
E♭
Gm
Dm
E♭
B♭/F
F7
mf
f
mp
molto rit.
E la fe - de che hai a - cce - so in noi. Sen - to che ci sal - ve -
G♭
A♭
B♭
rá.
p

SANTA BABY

Words and Music by
JOAN JAVITS, PHILIP SPRINGER
and TONY SPRINGER

© 1953 TRINITY MUSIC, INC.
Copyright Renewed in 1981 by PHILIP SPRINGER for the U.S.A.
Copyright Controlled for the World outside the U.S.A. by ALLEY MUSIC CORP. and TRIO MUSIC CO., INC.
All Rights Reserved

A7 D7 G Em A7 D7
slip a sa - ble un - der the tree for me. Been an aw - ful good girl,
lit - tle thing I real - ly do need; the deed to a plat - i - num mine,
G Em Am D7 G Em
San - ta Ba - by, so hur - ry down the chim - ney to - night.
San - ta hon - ey, so hur - ry down the chim - ney to - night.
Am7 D7 G Em A7 D7
San - ta Ba - by, a 'fif - ty - four con - vert - i - ble, too,
San - ta cut - ie, and fill my stock - ing with a du - plex
G Em A7 D7 G Em
light blue. I'll wait up for you, dear San - ta Ba - by, so
and cheques. Sign your X on the line, San - ta cut - ie, and

Am D7 G Em Am7 D7 G
hur - ry down the chim - ney to - night.
hur - ry down the chim - ney to - night.
B7 F♯m7/B B7 E7 Bm7
Think of all the fun I've missed. Think of all the fel - las that I
Come and trim my Christ - mas tree with some dec - o - ra - tions bought at
E7 A7 A9sus A7
have - n't kissed. Next year I could be just as good if
Tif - fa - ny. I real - ly do be - lieve in you. Let's
D Am7/D D7 G Em
you check off my Christ - mas list. San - ta Ba - by, I
see if you be - lieve in me. San - ta Ba - by, for -

A7
D7
G
Em
want a yacht and real - ly that's not a - lot.
got to men - tion one lit - tle thing, a ring!
A7
D7
G
Em
Been an an - gel all year, San - ta Ba - by, so
I don't mean on the phone, San - ta Ba - by, so
1.
Am
D7
G
Em
hur - ry down the chim - ney to - night.
hur - ry down the chim - ney to - night.
2.
Am7
D7
G
Em
Am7
D7(♭9)
G6/9

SANTA CLAUS IS COMIN' TO TOWN

Words by
HAVEN GILLESPIE

Music by
J. FRED COOTS

© 1934 (Renewed) EMI FEIST CATALOG INC. and HAVEN GILLESPIE MUSIC (c/o LARRY SPIER MUSIC, LLC) in the U.S.
All Rights for the World Outside of the U.S. Controlled by EMI FEIST CATALOG INC. (Publishing)
and ALFRED PUBLISHING CO., INC. (Print)
All Rights Reserved

C G7 C G7 C C/E E♭dim7
called on dear old San - ta Claus to see what I could see. He
bet - ter write your let - ter now and mail it right a - way, be -
G/D B♭dim7 Am7 D7 G G7(♯5)
took me to his work - shop and told his plans to me.
cause he's get - ting read - y his rein - deers and his sleigh.
So, you
Delicately
Chorus:
C C7 F/C Fm/C C C7 F Fm
bet - ter watch out, you bet - ter not cry. Bet - ter not pout, I'm tell - ing you why:
p
C Am F6 G7 C G7 C C7
San - ta Claus is com - in' to town. He's mak-ing a list and

F/C Fm/C C C7 F Fm C Am
check-ing it twice, gon - na find out who's naugh-ty and nice: San - ta Claus is
F6 G7 C Cdim7 C7 F
com - in' to town. He sees you when you're sleep - in'. He
mf
C7 F D7 G G♯dim7
knows when you're a - wake. He knows if you've been bad or good so be
Am7 D7 G G7(♯5) C C7 F/C Fm/C C C7
good for good-ness sake. Oh, you bet - ter watch out, you bet - ter not cry. Bet-ter not pout, I'm
p

Music box Chorus:
F Fm C Am F6 G7 C G7 C
tell-ing you why: San-ta Claus is com-in' to town. With lit-tle tin horns and
p
F C F Fm C G7
lit-tle toy drums, root-y toot-toots and rum-my tum-tums: San - ta Claus is com - in' to
8va
C G7 C F C
town. And cur-ly head dolls that tod-dle and coo, el - e-phants, boats and
(8va)
3
3
loco
p
F Fm C G7 C
kid-die cars too; San - ta Claus is com - in' to town.
8va
3

Cdim7 C7 F C7 F
— The kids in girl and boy-land will have a jub - i - lee. They're
(8va) loco
mf
D7 G G♯dim Am7 D7 G G7(♯5)
gon - na build a toy - land town all a - round the Christ - mas tree. So, you
p
C F C F Fm
bet - ter watch out, you bet - ter not cry, bet - ter not pout, I'm tell - ing you why:
C G7 C
San - ta Claus is com - in' to town.
8va
3

SILENT NIGHT

Words and Music by
JOSEPH MOHR and
FRANZ GRUBER

© 2009 ALFRED MUSIC PUBLISHING CO., INC.
All Rights Reserved

SLEIGH RIDE

Words by
MITCHELL PARISH

Music by
LEROY ANDERSON

© 1948, 1950 (Copyrights Renewed) EMI MILLS MUSIC, INC.
Rights for the Extended Renewal Term in the U.S. Controlled by WOODBURY MUSIC COMPANY and EMI MILLS MUSIC, INC.
Worldwide Print Rights Administered by ALFRED MUSIC PUBLISHING CO., INC.
All Rights Reserved

Gmaj7 G6 Am7 D7 Gmaj7 G6 Am7 D7
snow is fall - ing and friends are call - ing, "Yoo hoo." Come on, it's
Gmaj7 G6 Am7 D7 G C G C G
love - ly weath-er for a sleigh ride to - geth - er with you. Gid-dy -
C♯m7 F♯7 B
yap, gid - dy - yap, gid - dy - yap, let's go, let's look at the show,
C♯m7 F♯7 B F♯ B F♯ B
we're rid - ing in a won - der - land of snow. Gid - dy -

Bm7
E7
A
yap, gid - dy - yap, gid - dy - yap, it's grand, just hold - ing your hand.
Am7
D7
Am7/D
D7
We're glid - ing a - long with a song of a win - ter - y fair - y - land. Our cheeks are
Gmaj7
G6
Am7
D7
Gmaj7
G6
Am7
D7
nice and ros - y and com - fy co - zy are we. We're snug - gled
Gmaj7
G6
Am7
D7
G
B♭
D7
up to - geth - er like two birds of a feath - er would be. Let's take that

Gmaj7 G6 Am7 D7 Gmaj7 G6 Am7 D7
road be - fore us and sing a cho - rus or two. Come on, it's
1. To Interlude
Gmaj7 G6 Am7 D7 G C G C G D7
love - ly weath-er for a sleigh ride to-geth-er with you. There's a
2. Fine
Gmaj7 G6 Gmaj7 G6 Gmaj7 G
you.
dim.
p
f
Interlude:
Gmaj7
birth - day par - ty at the home of Farm - er Gray, it - 'll

G6
be the per - fect end - ing of a per - fect day. We'll be
G♯dim7
Am7
A♯dim7
G/B
B7
Em
C♯m7(♭5)
sing - ing the songs we love to sing with - out a sin - gle stop, at the
legato
B/F♯
C♯m7(♭5)
C♯m7
F♯7
B
G♯dim7
D7
fire - place while we watch the chest - nuts pop. Pop! Pop! Pop! There's a
Gmaj7
hap - py feel - ing noth - ing in the world can buy, when they

pass a - round the cof - fee and the pump - kin
G6
G♯dim7
Am7
A♯dim7
pie. It - 'll near - ly be like a pic - ture print by
legato
G/B
B7
Em
A7
D
C/D
Cur - ri - er and Ives. These won - der - ful
D
C/D
D
C/D
D
C/D
D7
D.S. 𝄋 al Fine
things are the things we re - mem - ber all through our lives! Just hear those

THE TWELVE DAYS OF CHRISTMAS

TRADITIONAL ENGLISH

© 2009 ALFRED MUSIC PUBLISHING CO., INC.
All Rights Reserved

D7
C
G
D7
G
three French_ hens, two tur - tle doves, and a par - tridge_ in a pear tree. 4. On the
Verse 4:
D7
G
D7
fourth day of Christ - mas, my true love sent to me four call - ing birds, three French_ hens,
C
G
D7
G
Verse 5:
two tur - tle doves, and a par - tridge_ in a pear tree. 5. On the fifth day of Christ-mas, my
D7
G
A7
D
D7
G
true love sent to me five gold - en rings, four___ call - ing birds,

C A7 D G C G D7 G
three French Hens, two__ tur - tle doves, and a par - tridge_ in a pear tree. 6. On the
Verse 6:
D7 G D7 G A7
sixth day of Christ - mas, my true love sent to me six geese a - lay - ing, five gold - en
D D7 G C A7 D
rings, four__ call - ing birds, three French hens, two__ tur - tle doves, and a
G C G D7 G
Verse 7:
D7 G
par - tridge_ in a pear tree. 7. On the sev-enth day of Christ-mas, my true love sent to me

D7
G
A7
D
D7
sev - en swans a - swim-ming, six geese a - lay - ing, five gold - en rings,
G
C
A7
D
G
C
G
D7
four__ call - ing birds, three French hens, two__ tur - tle doves, and a par - tridge_ in a pear
G
Verse 8:
D7
G
D7
tree. 8. On the eighth day of Christ - mas, my true love sent to me eight maids a - milk - ing,
G
A7
D
D7
sev - en swans a - swim-ming, six geese a - lay - ing, five gold - en rings,

G C A7 D G C G D7
four__ call - ing birds, three French hens, two__ tur - tle doves, and a par - tridge_ in a pear
G Verse 9: D7 G D7
tree. 9. On the ninth day of Christ - mas, my true love sent to me nine la - dies danc-ing,
G A7
eight maids a - milk - ing, sev - en swans a - swim-ming, six geese a - lay - ing, five gold - en
D D7 G C A7 D
rings, four__ call - ing birds, three French hens, two__ tur - tle doves, and a

Verse 10:
G C G D7 G D7 G
par - tridge in a pear tree. 10. On the tenth day of Christ-mas, my true love sent to me
D7
tens lords a - leap - ing, nine la - dies danc - ing, eight maids a - milk - ing, sev - en swans a - swim - ming,
G A7 D D7 G
six geese a - lay - ing, five gold - en rings, four call - ing birds,
C A7 D G C G D7 G
three French hens, two tur - tle doves, and a par - tridge in a pear tree. 11. On the e -

Verse 11:
D7
G
D7
lev-enth day of Christ-mas, my true love sent to me___ e - lev - en pip - ers pip - ing, ten lords a - leap-ing,
nine la - dies danc-ing, eight maids a - milk - ing, sev - en swans a - swim-ming, six geese a - lay - ing,
G
A7
D
D7
G
C
five gold - en rings, four___ call - ing birds, three French hens,
A7
D
G
C
G
D7
G
Verse 12:
two___ tur - tle doves, and a par - tridge_ in a pear tree. 12. On the twelfth day of Christ-mas, my

D7 G D7
true love sent to me twelve drum-mers drum-ming, e - lev - en pip - ers pip - ing, ten lords a - leap-ing,
nine la - dies danc-ing, eight maids a - milk-ing, sev - en swans a - swim-ming, six geese a - lay - ing,
G A7 D D7 G C
five gold - en rings, four call - ing birds, three French hens,
A7 D G C G D7 G
two tur - tle doves, and a par - tridge in a pear tree.
rit.

WE WISH YOU A MERRY CHRISTMAS

TRADITIONAL ENGLISH FOLK SONG

© 2009 ALFRED MUSIC PUBLISHING CO., INC.
All Rights Reserved

D Em A D G D Em7
tid - ings we bring to you and your kin; good tid - ings for
D G/B C D7 G G
1.2.3. 4.
Chrst - mas and a Hap - py New Year. 2. Oh, 3. We 4. We Year. 5. We
C A D
wish you a Mer - ry Christ - mas, we wish you a Mer - ry Christ - mas, we
G B7 G
wish you a Mer - ry Christ - mas and a hap - py New Year.

From THE POLAR EXPRESS

WHEN CHRISTMAS COMES TO TOWN

Lyrics by
GLEN BALLARD

Music by
ALAN SILVESTRI

© 2004 HAZEN MUSIC, JOBANALA MUSIC and AEROSTATION CORPORATION
All Rights on Behalf of HAZEN MUSIC Administered by WB MUSIC CORP.
All Rights Reserved

E♭sus E♭ Fm7 B♭7/D E♭ E♭/G A♭ E♭/G
find me Christ-mas Eve. I guess that San - ta's bus - y 'cause he's nev - er come a - round. I
Fm7 B♭7sus E♭ E♭sus E♭ E♭sus E♭
think of him when Christ - mas comes to town. The
mp
E♭sus E♭ E♭sus E♭ E♭sus E♭
best time of the year, when ev - 'ry - one comes home; with all this Christ-mas cheer it's
E♭sus E♭ Fm7 B♭/D E♭ E♭/G A♭ E♭/G
hard to be a - lone. Put - ting up the Christ-mas tree with friends who come a - round, it's

Fm7
Fm7/B♭
E♭sus
E♭
so much fun when Christ - mas comes to town.
cresc.
C♭
D♭/C♭
B♭m7
E♭m
Pres - ents for the chil - dren wrapped in red and green;
mf
C♭
D♭/C♭
B♭m7
E♭m
all the things I've heard a - bout but nev - er real - ly seen.
Fm7(♭5)
/E♭
B♭7/D
E♭m
/D
G♭/D♭
No one will be sleep - ing on the night of Christ - mas Eve, hop - ing

F♯m7 B7 Fm7 B♭7sus B♭7 E♭ E♭sus E♭ E♭sus E♭
San-ta's on his way.
mp
E♭sus E♭ E♭sus E♭ E♭sus E♭ Fm7 /E♭ B♭/D E♭ E♭/G A♭ E♭/G
Fm7 Fm7/B♭ E♭sus E♭ C♭ D♭/C♭
Pres-ents for the chil - dren
mf
B♭m7 E♭m C♭ D♭/C♭ B♭m7 E♭m
wrapped in red and green; all the things I've heard a-bout but nev-er real - ly seen.

Fm7(♭5) /E♭ B♭7/D E♭m /D G♭/D♭ F♯m7 B7
No one will be sleep - ing on the night of Christ-mas Eve, hop-ing San - ta's on his
Fm7 B♭7sus B♭7 E♭ E♭sus E♭ E♭sus E♭
way. When San - ta's sleigh bells ring, I lis - ten all a-round. The
mp
E♭sus E♭ E♭sus E♭ Fm7 B♭/D
her - ald an - gels sing; I nev - er hear a sound. And all the dreams of chil - dren, once
E♭ E♭/G A♭ E♭/G Fm7 Fm7/B♭ Bdim7 Cm F9
lost, will all be found. That's all I want when Christ-mas comes to town.

Fm7
Fm7/B♭
That's all I want when Christ - mas comes to
E♭ E♭sus E♭
E♭sus E♭
E♭sus E♭
E♭sus E♭
town.
E♭sus E♭
E♭sus E♭
E♭sus E♭
E♭sus E♭
E♭sus E♭
E♭sus E♭
E♭sus E♭
E♭sus E♭
p

WEXFORD CAROL

Traditional,
Arranged by DAVID DOWNES

Very slowly, rubato throughout ♩ = 60

© 2006 LIFFEY PUBLISHING LTD, Dublin 2, Ireland
All Rights Reserved Used by Permission

Beth - le - hem up - on that morn there was a bless - ed Mes - si - ah born. Near
Ooo.
Ooo.
Beth - le - hem did shep - herds keep their flocks of lambs and
mp Beth - le - hem did shep - herds keep their flocks of lambs and
feed - ing sheep; To whom God's an - gels did ap - pear, which
feed - ing sheep; To whom God's an - gels did ap - pear,

put the shep - herds in great fear. "A - rise and go." the
mp Ooo. "A - rise and go." the
mf
an - gels said, "To Beth - le - hem, be not a - fraid; for
an - gels said, "Beth - le - hem, be not a - fraid; p for
there you'll find, this hap - py morn, a prince - ly babe, sweet Je - sus born."
there you'll find, this hap - py morn." Ooo.

Ooo.
With
Ooo.
thank - ful heart and joy - ful mind, the shep - herds went, that
f Thank - ful heart and joy - ful mind, shep - herds went, that
Ahh.
babe to find, and as God's an - gel had fore - told, they
babe to find, as God's an - gel had fore - told,

did our Sav - ior Christ be - hold. With - in a man - ger He was laid, and
mp Ooo.
p Ooo.
by His side the vir - gin maid, as long fore - told up -
Ooo.
As long fore - told up -
mp
on that morn there was a bless - ed Mes - si - ah born.
on that morn.
Ooo.
pp

WINTER WONDERLAND

Words by
DICK SMITH

Music by
FELIX BERNARD

© 1934 (Renewed) WB MUSIC CORP.
All Rights Reserved

E♭ Fm7/B♭ E♭maj7 B♭7 E♭ Cm
heav - en of dia - monds shine down thru the night; two hearts are thrill - in' in
F7 B♭7 E♭maj7 Cm7 E7 B♭7
spite of the chill in the weath - er.
E♭ Fm7/B♭ E♭ Fm7/B♭ E♭ Fm7/B♭
Love knows no sea - son, love knows no clime, ro - mance can blos - som
E♭maj7 B♭7 E♭ Cm F7 B♭7
an - y old time. Here in the o - pen, we're walk - in' and hop - in' to -

Refrain:
E♭maj7
Cm
E7
B♭7
E♭
geth - er!
Sleigh - bells ring, are you
p - f
B♭7
lis - t'nin'? In the lane, snow is glis - t'nin'. A
F7
B♭7
beau - ti - ful sight, we're hap - py to - night, walk - in' in a win - ter won - der -
E♭
land! Gone a - way is the blue - bird, here to

B♭7
stay is a new bird.
He sings a love song
He's sing - ing a song
as
F7
B♭7
E♭
we go a - long,
walk - in' in a win - ter won - der - land!
G
D7
G
D7
In the mead - ow, we can build a snow - man,
then pre - tend that he is Par - son
and pre - tend that he's a cir - cus
G
B♭
F7
B♭
Brown.
clown.
He'll say, "Are you mar - ried?" We'll say, "No, man! But
We'll have lots of fun with Mis - ter Snow - man, un -

C7
F7
B♭7
E♭
you can do the job when you're in town!"
til the oth - er kid - dies knock 'em down!
Lat - er on, we'll con -
When it snows, ain't it
B♭7
spire, as we dream by the fire, to
thrill - in', though your nose gets a chill - in'? We'll
F7
B♭7
face un - a - fraid the plans that we made, walk - in' in a win - ter won - der -
frol - ic and play the Es - ki - mo way, walk - in' in a win - ter won - der -
1.
E♭
B♭7
land! Sleigh - bells
2.
E♭
land!

YOU'RE A MEAN ONE, MR. GRINCH

(from *How the Grinch Stole Christmas*)

Lyrics by
DR. SEUSS

Music by
ALBERT HAGUE

© 1966 (Renewed) TED GEISEL PUBLISHING and ALBERT HAGUE
All Rights Controlled by EMI ROBBINS CATALOG INC. (Publishing) and ALFRED MUSIC PUBLISHING CO., INC. (Print)
All Rights Reserved

Verse 2:
You're a monster, Mr. Grinch!
Your heart's an empty hole.
Your brain is full of spiders,
You've got garlic in your soul, Mr. Grinch!
I wouldn't touch you with a
Thirty-nine-and-one-half-foot pole.

Verse 3:
You're a foul one, Mr. Grinch!
You're a nasty-wasty skunk!
Your heart is full of unwashed socks,
Your soul is full of gunk, Mr. Grinch!
The three words that best describe you
Are as follows and I quote:
Stink! - Stank! - Stunk!

Verse 4:
You're a vile one, Mr. Grinch!
You have termites in your smile.
You have all the tender sweetness
Of a seasick crocodile, Mr. Grinch!
(Spoken:) And given the choice between the two of you
I'd take the seasick crocodile.

Verse 5:
You're a rotter, Mr. Grinch!
You're the king of sinful sots.
Your heart's a dead tomato
Spotched with moldy, purple spots, Mr. Grinch…
(Spoken:) Your soul is an appalling dumpheap overflowing with the most disgraceful assortment of deplorable rubbish imaginable, mangled up in
…Tangled-up knots.

Verse 6:
You nauseate me, Mr. Grinch!
With a nauseous, super naus.
You're a crooked jerkey jockey
And you drive a crooked hoss, Mr. Grinch!
(Spoken:) You're a three-decker Sauerkraut and toadstool sandwich
…with arsenic sauce.

WIZARDS IN WINTER

(Instrumental)

Music by
PAUL O'NEILL and ROBERT KINKEL

© 2004 WARNER-TAMERLANE PUBLISHING CORP., PAUL O'NEILL PUBLISHING and ROBERT STELLAR PUBLISHING
All Rights Administered by WARNER-TAMERLANE PUBLISHING CORP.
All Rights Reserved

Em
E sus2 sus4
Em
D/E
G
D/G
G
B
Em
B/E
Em
B
Em
E sus2 sus4
Em
D/E
G
D/G
G
B
Em
B/E
Em
B
Em
E sus2 sus4
Em
D/E
G
D/G
G
B
Em
B/E
Em
B

N.C.
f
Em
D/E
Em
D/E
Em
D/E
Em
D/E
Em
B
cresc.

Em
Esus2/sus4
Em
D/E
G
D/G
G
B
Em
B/E
Em
B
Em
Esus2/sus4
Em
D/E
G
D/G
G
B
Em
B/E
Em
B
dim.
8va
loco
mp
Em
mf

8va
(8va)
B
f
Em
Esus2 sus4
Em
D/E
G
D/G
G
B

Em
B/E
Em
B
Em
Esus2/sus4
Em
D/E
G
D/G
G
B
Em
B/E
Em
B
Em
Esus2/sus4
Em
D/E
G
D/G
G
B
Em
Esus2/sus4
Em
D/E
G
D/G
G
B
Em
Esus2/sus4
Em
D/E
G
D/G
G
B

Em
D/F♯
G
D/A
Em
D/F♯
G
D/A
Em
G
Em
G
Em
G
Em
G
Em
cresc.
f
sfz